The Learning Annex

presents

Making Money in Real Estate

The Learning Annex

presents

Making Money in Real Estate

A Smarter Approach to Real Estate Investing

Robert Shemin

WILEY

John Wiley & Sons, Inc.

For general information on our other products and services please contact our Customer Care Department within the United States at (800) 762-2974, outside the United States at (317) 572-3993 or fax (317) 572-4002.

Wiley also publishes its books in a variety of electronic formats. Some content that appears in print may not be available in electronic books. For more information about Wiley products, visit our web site at *www.Wiley.com.*

ISBN 0-471-69746-X

Printed in the United States of America

10 9 8 7 6 5 4 3 2

contents

PART III EXPANDING YOUR KNOWLEDGE BASE

preface

Property is the fruit of labor; property is desirable; it is a positive good in the world.

That some should be rich shows that others may become rich and, hence, is just encouragement to industry and enterprise.

—Abraham Lincoln

For more than 12 years, I have been an active, full-time real estate investor. In those years, I have built a fortune and have retired twice—the first time at age 32. I have bought and sold 700 properties, been included in countless transactions, and have taught thousands of people around the world the techniques to make them wealthy. I have written six bestselling books, most of which have become the top real estate books in the United States. But although my books sell well, I made more money from one real estate deal last year than from all my book royalties combined over the past four years. Where is the money? In real estate. Above and beyond the financial rewards of real estate, I stay involved for another important reason: It is fun. I am having a wonderful time!

Each year, many people ask me why I write books. I wrote the first books to help me. Those earlier writings cataloged the answers to questions I had as an investor: How do I find good deals? What type of real estate should I invest in? How do I structure little-to-no-money and no-risk deals? And, finally, how do people make all of this money with real estate? In addition, I found myself spending a lot of time telling others the same things, and answering their questions. Eventually, I wrote a report and asked them to read it.

I write books because I love to teach. I suppose that you could call me a teacher at heart. I also love to write. But most of all, I love helping other people achieve their dreams and goals. For all these reasons, I began to lead workshops and training programs. They allow me to bring together more people at one time, to teach and train them how to become successful real estate investors and to make changes that will improve their financial, personal, and professional lives. It is satisfying to help other people.

Recently, at a conference, I was approached by a young couple who had a first edition of one of my earlier books. They humbly asked if I would inscribe it for them. As I took the book, I noticed that it had been well used: It was worn, with bent pages, underlining, and annotations. The couple thanked me for helping them become financially independent, for helping them to change their lives. But it was they who took action and made it happen. After signing the book and posing for a picture with them, I was overcome with gratitude and satisfaction.

From a financial standpoint, I do not have to do any more real estate deals. But because I love what I do, I will not stop. It is too rewarding, personally, professionally, and financially. In short, I am addicted. But I also love giving back; doing so gives me great pleasure. So I donate most of the profits and proceeds from my book sales to various charities. And at least once a year, I take one of my homes and pass it on to a family without a home. Why? We live in the wealthiest, most powerful country in the world. It is a shame that any child or mother should have to sleep on the street or in a shelter. It is my deep belief that whatever we are doing, it is important to take some of our time, talents, and gifts and share them with other people. It is impossible to describe the enjoyment and heartfelt joy I feel when I am helping other people get started, watching them experience success and, then, in turn, going forward to help others. In short, I am planting a seed.

I ask all of you reading this book, especially beginning investors, to make a commitment now to give something back. Help a homeless family as you prosper in this business. Although I have given away several homes anonymously, I have also gone on talk shows to publicize my home-giving, with the hope of inspiring some of you to do the same. My primary goal in all of these efforts is to one day never see a child in the United States living in a homeless shelter or on the street.

I also want to see you enjoy some of the same or similar success that I have been blessed with: financial security, peace of mind, and a satisfying life. To that end, this book will teach you the principles, techniques, strategies, and how-to's of making money in real estate. It is then up to you to go out and make it happen. You must take action, like the couple I just described. You must make the commitment to put all this information into practice.

I wish you luck and good fortune as you begin your real estate investing career.

part I

laying a knowledge foundation

chapter 1

getting started right

The individual who wants to reach the top in business must appreciate the might of the force of habit—and must understand that practices are what create habits. He must be quick to break those habits that can break him— and faster to adopt those practices that will become the habits that help him achieve the success he desires.

—J. Paul Getty

When I started in real estate, I thought there was only one way to buy real estate: Borrow money, buy property, put my name on the title, rent it, put up with tenants, have the tenants pay off the mortgage and other costs, and make money over time. With luck, I would make money every month.

Then I learned how to wholesale property, fix it up and sell it, or lease-option it. I also learned that I did not have to use my own money or credit to acquire property. Most people, including myself sometimes, have no hands-on experience in the subject matter about which they are giving advice. You should seek advice only from experts. Even my mother would say, "Robert, this no-money-down stuff, I don't buy it; I don't believe it can be true." Still, to this day, every time I go to my mother's house for dinner, she says, "Robert, I've seen you on TV and have looked at your books in the stores. Why do you keep telling people they can buy property without using their own money or credit? Stop it!" She still will not believe me. She's an expert at being a mom, but she has

robert's success tip

Who do you take advice from? (1) People who have no actual knowledge or experience on the subject matter? (2) Those who have tried and failed? Or (3) subject-matter experts with years of demonstrable experience who have successful track records? You decide who your advisors/mentors will be. Hopefully, they will come from category 3.

not done any real estate investing. But it's true: For the last 400 properties that I have bought, sold, and made money on, I have not used one penny of my own money or one point of my own credit. You will learn many ways to do that, too.

The concepts and systems I present here work for everything: houses, duplexes, land, commercial buildings, apartment buildings, trailer parks, development conversion projects; small properties, big ones, cheap ones, and expensive ones. There is no difference between a $1 million property and a $100,000 property; the process and paperwork for buying and selling them are exactly the same.

As a full-time real estate investor, I have bought or sold approximately 700 properties in the last five or six years. At one time, I had more than 300 tenants, living in properties I owned and managed for years. Today, I still own and manage more than 150 rental properties. I constantly buy, flip, lease-option, develop, rehab, and broker properties.

I decided that working at a job for 50 years and waiting for retirement was not for me. I recently purchased a beautiful penthouse condo in South Beach, Florida, and now I get to live where many people only vacation. I am now wholesaling expensive properties there, and am active as well in Los Angeles, California, Las Vegas, Nevada, and in Costa Rica and Latin America. Once you learn the concepts and systems—the how-to's—you, too, can go anywhere. My students have demonstrated that the concepts and systems in this book work in even the most expensive real estate markets in the world: Manhattan and San Francisco. They will work in your town—or 25 miles up the road.

HOW ONE MAN CHANGED MY MIND— AND MY LIFE

I am from Nashville, Tennessee, a gathering place where talented people go to make it big. Sometimes one becomes an "overnight success," as did

Garth Brooks, my neighbor for five years—but only after getting kicked out of every record company, and singing and playing guitar on street corners for 12 years. I've experienced that kind of overnight success, too.

Approximately 12 years ago, I did not know a thing about real estate and did not want to. I was a financial consultant working for a New York financial planning firm. Our high-net-worth clients had to have between $3 and $10 million just to qualify to invest with us. Again, I had no interest in real estate and no desire to get involved in it. That is, until one day, when I was sent by my firm to visit an older couple living in a small town outside Nashville.

Upon my arrival, I was shocked. I noticed a beat-up pickup truck parked outside a dumpy old office. Reluctantly, I got out of my car and knocked on the front door. An elderly gentleman greeted me warmly. I noticed that he and his wife did not have computers; nor did they understand advanced finance—they did not even know what a term like "return on investment" meant. "Obviously, you are not qualified to work with my firm," I said as I stood up to leave. The old gentlemen replied, "Come over here, Sonny." He picked up a large, worn accounting book, paused, then said, "When I was working about 25 years ago and making hardly any money, I started buying little houses without using any of my own money. I'd fix them up, rent them, and sell them." He then opened his book, the kind with old ledger sheets and lines crisscrossing the pages. He kept (and still does) all of his own records using just that book and a pencil. I learned he owned 125 houses, all paid for. He then showed me he had a $65,000 monthly net income, after all expenses. He explained that he and his wife go on vacation for six months every year. Then he looked me in the eye and sternly asked, "Robert, how's your job?"

Suddenly, young cocky Robert became very interested in this man's profession: real estate. In the back of my mind, I thought, "If this 80-year-old guy can do it, I've got a chance! If I did only one-tenth of what he did, I would be better off than I am now." I also found out this man still picks up rent checks every month and closes more deals. He certainly does not have to. But for him, real estate is fun.

QUICK TO PLAN, SLOW TO ACT

Needless to say, my interest was piqued. I followed him around for several months during this time. I interviewed 200 investors and some 300 tenants. I put together a big plan for my real estate business. And guess what I did with the plan for several months afterward? Nothing! As the expression goes, "I was thinkin' about it. I was a fixin' to do somethin.'" That went on for about eight months. During that time, I looked at about 150 properties. Of those, at least 50 were great deals, but I did not understand wholesaling and lease optioning. I had no system, no mentor. I was scared and so took no action. Because of fear and ignorance, I let millions in real estate profits pass me by.

robert's success tip

When has fear ever served you? Write down what you're scared of, and why, then write down actions you can implement to face and conquer your fear.

Finally, I did make an offer on a duplex, and it was accepted. But that scared me, too. How would I close on it? I borrowed money and bought that duplex. At that time, my written plan was to buy 12 duplexes and retire. I figured each one would draw from $300 to $500 a month in cash flow, which I could live on. It was that old couple's success that got me started.

TAKING ACTION: ONE DUPLEX TURNS INTO A DOZEN

Because I have a form of dyslexia, I struggle doing many of the things that come easily for others, and that some people take for granted. For example, I cannot follow simple directions to put together a four-year-old's toy. I am unable to read maps. Certain mathematical things I cannot do. And even though I have rehabbed at least 500 houses, I know *absolutely nothing* about construction or repairs. When contractors talk about roof trusses, drywall, and wires, it is as if they were speaking Chinese or Greek. Their language simply makes no sense in my brain.

I tell you this so you'll understand when I say that after closing on my first duplex, I became hopelessly lost trying to find my duplex. For a day and a half, I drove around Hermitage, Tennessee, looking for it. They all looked the same. In frustration, I finally called the broker and asked, "I can't find the property I just closed on. Where is it?" I was so embarrassed. He came to meet me and drove me to it.

Fortunately, after getting help, I did find my first duplex, and rented it out. Then I bought 12 more duplexes. After a year and a half, I quit my job and retired. For a year, I did not do anything, because I had approximately $4,000 to $5,000 of tax-free money coming in every month. Then I thought, "Gee, if it works with 12 duplexes, it has to

robert's system tip

Instead of learning one way to make money in real estate, learn all of them. You may not use them all, but you'll be able to pick a few from among them to get started.

work with 20 or 25; and if it works with 25, it should work with 50; and if it works with 50, it has to work with 100, 200, and 300 properties. (Now I do have help: one person who helps me manage all of my properties, and a part-time secretary.)

WHY REAL ESTATE INVESTING

Maybe you want to buy your own home and learn how to save thousands of dollars on the transaction. Maybe you realize there is no job security in the United States—what with layoffs, downsizing, reengineering, and forced early retirements—so you want to run your own business. Even if you have a great job and things are going well, even if you are wealthy and successful, I challenge you to begin investing in real estate.

Think about it: You live somewhere right now. If you pay rent, you are probably making someone else wealthy. You are contributing to that person's investments and security, not yours. You pay your rent on time and thank your landlord, but at the end of the year, you have nothing to show for it except 12 canceled checks. If you own a home, you are already a real estate investor. You probably know somebody—a friend, a relative, a coworker, a grandparent, an uncle or an aunt—who has made a lot of money in real estate, often by accident. Most people spend 40 to 50 hours a week stressed out, working to make $40,000 a year, and then, with one real estate deal, they make $40,000 almost by accident in a short amount of time.

"Will you be successful as a real estate investor?" Yes, you will if you possess the following three components, which combine into a formula for success:

1. **Belief and desire**

2. **Basic knowledge and information**

3. **Persistent action**

This book can give you all of the basic information that you need to get started. Make this book the catalyst to get you started the right way and to find within yourself the desire to succeed. I hope this book encourages you to start taking persistent actions toward becoming a real estate investor with various sources of income.

To further motivate you, in Chapter 2 I explain why real estate investing is one of the best wealth builders in the universe.

why real estate is the best wealth builder in the universe

Act as if it were impossible to fail.
—Dorothea Brande

In Chapter 1, I introduced you to the three-part formula successful people and, specifically, real estate investors, follow to ensure their success. Before I explain how and why real estate is the best wealth builder in the universe, I want to begin here by delving into that formula a little deeper.

1. *Belief and desire.* Success always starts in the same place, with belief and desire. According to research, it has been determined that the primary indicators of all success are, one, belief in self—in this case believing you can succeed in real estate—and, two, a burning desire to be and do different things. Not education, not inheritance, not privilege or good looks—simply, your belief and desire.

2. *Basic knowledge and information.* This, believe it or not, is the easy part. Knowledge is abundant. You are beginning to

consider this

As you set out, ask yourself:

- Is my desire to achieve success in real estate, along with my belief in myself, greater than the fear that will hold me back?
- Do I sincerely believe that I deserve more and can expect more if I truly believe and desire?

educate yourself by reading this book. The next step is to find a qualified and experienced mentor. For now, you can think of me as your first mentor. I and your future investor mentors can help you to avoid trial-and-error mistakes as you build your real estate career. But let's face it, all the belief and desire, coupled with rock-solid knowledge, mean nothing if you don't implement the third component in the success formula.

3. *Persistent action.*   This means taking consistent action.

This is the formula for success in any endeavor, whether it be personal in nature, career-oriented, or finance-related.

I hope that I have convinced you that you, too, can succeed as a real estate investor, at least enough to follow me as we get down to the nitty-gritty.

ADVANTAGES OF INVESTING IN REAL ESTATE

Simply put, investing in real estate is the best wealth builder in the universe because *everyone needs a place to live.* Historically, this is borne out in numbers, because real estate values usually go up over time. I can assure you that any real estate you have will probably double or triple, perhaps even quadruple in value in the next 20 years. If you are in a "hot" market, it might even go up 10 to 20 times. So when is the right time to get into real estate investing? Yesterday.

Here, in brief, are five powerful reasons why investing in real estate can lead to wealth for you:

1. *Real estate increases your net worth.*   One of the primary advantages of real estate is that your net worth can instantly increase when you buy a property below market value. For example, if you find a property that is worth $500,000 and a motivated seller who is willing to let it go for $300,000, you put it under contract for $300,000 (about 60 percent of its worth), then borrow all $300,000, close the deal, and become the owner of this property. You borrowed all of the money to make this happen; you did not use your own. The minute you own this property, your bank and your financial statement say you have an asset worth $500,000 and a $300,000 loan against it. Congratulations. Your net worth just went up $200,000.

Here is a more conservative example. In my first real estate deal, I bought a duplex that was worth $60,000 for $40,000—not a home-run deal, certainly not a grand slam—but as soon as I bought the duplex, my net worth went up $20,000. Property value ($60,000) minus property cost ($40,000) equals gain in net worth ($20,000).

This concept is hard for most Americans to understand because usually when they buy something big (e.g., a new car, television, jewelry, stereo), their net worth goes down instantly. The $30,000 car I bought goes down in value to $20,000; therefore, my net worth decreases by $10,000. However, if you buy real estate correctly, your net worth goes up because it appreciates over time, unlike most items that depreciate.

2. *Real estate generates income from holding properties.*   Rental property (a house, commercial property, or an apartment building) is unique because your tenants pay off your debt on that real estate. If you own rental property with $500 monthly mortgage payments and $800 monthly rental income, you end up with a cash flow of $300, which is extra money in your pocket. The cash will likely be tax-free because of depreciation and write-offs.

Your tenants actually pay off your mortgage debt and, in 10 to 30 years (depending on the term of the loan), that debt will disappear and your net worth will go up again.

3. *With real estate, you can pay less than what the property is worth.*   By looking for deals, you can buy real estate that is priced at 20 to 50 percent

robert's tip

Residual income creates happiness (RICH) is the concept that you, your family, and your estate (after you die) will accrue from residual income because the rent keeps coming in.

of what it is worth. This means you seek $100,000 properties that you can buy for, say, $70,000. Compare that with the stock market. Can you find stock that is worth $100 and pay $70 for it? No. You pay $70, the market value, then pray it goes up to $100. It could hold at $70 for a year, then go up, or it could go down because that's the nature of the stock market. You cannot buy stocks below market value like you can real estate.

4. *Real estate offers tax advantages.*   The fourth big advantage of real estate investing is how it affects your tax obligations. If you have a traditional job with a traditional paycheck, you are entitled to very few tax write-offs or deductions. However, in real estate or any business you own, you can write off a wide array of expenses, including phone calls and a portion of your business meals. Owning real estate provides the opportunity to write off most of your mortgage interest and property depreciation.

5. *You do not need cash or credit to get into real estate.*   In the stock market, you require most or all of your cash up front to purchase stocks. If you want to buy a $100 stock, you have to pay $100 cash. Some banks or brokerage houses will lend you half of the money to buy stock, but you will still have to come up with the other half.

In real estate investing, if you find a property selling for $70,000 that is worth $100,000, you can borrow the entire $70,000. If you have good credit, almost any bank or mortgage company will lend you 70 percent ($70,000) to buy the $100,000 property. If you do not have cash or good credit, you can find hard money-lenders who will lend money—in return for charging a high interest rate. They will lend you $70,000 for a property worth $100,000 without caring if you pay them back, because if you do not pay them, they take your property.

In any business or investment, especially real estate, you can use either your own money (YOM) or other people's money (OPM). *Owner's terms* is an example of OPM. If you buy a house and the owner lends you money to purchase it, you are using the owner's money instead of having to go to a bank.

What if you do not have enough money or credit to invest, but have enough knowledge to be a successful real estate investor?

Then look for investors (i.e., people with money or good credit) who can borrow at great rates. These investors may have a lot of cash or retirement accounts that they are tired of putting into stocks and are seeking other ways to invest. You might convince them to invest with you if you have a good business plan and have already had some business success. Investors put in the money while you put in the knowledge and time.

More on these and other advantages of real estate in a moment, but first a few words about real estate versus the stock market.

REAL ESTATE VERSUS THE STOCK MARKET

Have you ever tried to get in the stock market to make money? It can work; however, you have to buy a stock at the price it sells for on the day you buy. Let's say the price of a company's stock is $100 a share. If you want to buy it, you have to pay $100 and pray it goes up. If it goes to $120 in a year, you've made $20 for every $100 you spent on that stock. That's a 20 percent return on your investment, which is a great return.

You must be able to take into account that, historically, the stock market has between about a 9 and 13 percent annualized return—an average of 11 percent over the past 40 or 50 years. So if you're making 11 percent or more, you're doing great in the stock market. Unfortunately, for many, their stocks have gone down 10, 20, even 30 percent in the past few years.

However, to buy that $100 stock, you have to give the bank or brokerage firm (or whoever makes the transaction for you) a commission, plus you have to determine where that $100 comes from. If you have excellent credit, the brokerage may lend you half of the $100 and you still have to put up $50 of your own cash. That's what some people do when they invest in the stock market. Considering commissions and borrowing expenses, how much are you really making on the appreciation of that stock?

Real estate, in comparison, makes for a better, long-term investment because of the features that make it unique.

WHAT MAKES REAL ESTATE UNIQUE

If you're serious about your money and serious about investing, you'll consider all the advantages of real estate investing that don't exist in other forms of investing.

Contract Real Estate for Less Than Its Value

Houses worth $100,000 can actually be found for $75,000 or $80,000. Some real estate worth $1 million can be found for $700,000; other properties worth $450,000 can be found for $350,000. You can contract to buy a property and control it immediately, even though you haven't given the seller money for it yet. Then, between 30 and 100 days later, you go to the closing and give the seller the agreed-upon price. You borrow money to pay for the property, then close on it, and, voilà, you own it.

Make an Infinite Return on Investment

If you find a house worth $1 million for $500,000 and your credit isn't great, there are some lenders who would lend you $500,000 for a property worth $1 million. In fact, they'd hope you'd miss a payment so they could take over the $1 million property for $500,000.

These lenders are called *hard moneylenders*. They don't pay attention to your credit; they care about the asset, the property itself, when they make their lending decisions. If it's 60 to 75 percent loan to value (see accompanying explanation), they might lend the funds regardless of your credit. Some of the big banks and mortgage companies make loans to people who have been in bankruptcy, who have made late payments, who have bad credit, and so on. They may still lend you 60 to 80 percent of

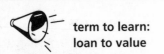

term to learn:
loan to value

Loan to value is a term used by real estate investors and lenders to indicate the ratio of debt or borrowed money compared to the value of a property.

If the house is worth $200,000 and the loan or mortgage is $200,000, then there is a 100 percent loan to value. Many conventional or regular lenders will lend 80 to 100 percent loan to value to home buyers who are going to live in the home. These are called *owner-occupied loans* since the loan is to someone who is going to live in the home. An *investor loan* is a loan to someone who is not going to live in the property. These loans are typically 65 to 85 percent loan to value. However, there are some 90 to 100 percent loan-to-value loans for investors.

All loans depend on three things: *collateral,* the value and type of asset or property; *credit,* the credit history of the borrower; and *income,* or the borrower's ability to repay the loan.

the sale price on these properties. That's why you can find a property worth $100,000 and get it for $75,000, then borrow that $75,000 without putting your own money into the property. You rent the property for $1,000 a month, and your payment on the $75,000 you borrowed is $700 a month. After all of the expenses—taxes, insurance, vacancies, repairs, and overhead—you make some cash each month. Let's say you make $100 profit a month from the rent after paying all of the expenses. You've still invested zero in the property. Your return is infinite: $X for $0 invested.

Do you realize that this *wouldn't* work if you were buying stocks or gold or any other investment? With real estate, you potentially have an infinite return on your investment. If you make only $1 because of unforeseen circumstances, your turnaround investment is still infinite because none of your own money is invested.

Appreciate Real Estate Appreciation

Stocks certainly don't appreciate every year, especially if they're affected by an accounting scandal such as those experienced by Enron or MCI WorldCom in 2001–2002. Stocks can go from $80 a share down to $1 a share or less while, in most areas, real estate appreciates from 4 to 6 percent a year. It goes up even more in certain hot markets. Investing in real estate can bring you the greatest gains in your life if you can hang in there and stick it out. Think about what real estate in your own community was selling for 15 years ago compared with now, then

 **think about it**

You make most of your money in real estate when you find, contract, and/or buy the property. When you find and contract a house worth $380,000 today for $310,000 from a motivated seller, then you have a locked-in profit of $70,000 (i.e., $380,000 – $310,000 = $70,000). You can sell it or keep it and hope it appreciates in value even more. Some skeptics say you can't find houses for 15 to 30 percent below what they are worth today. They are right—*they* can't because they are skeptical. Those who go out and search do find great deals. Hundreds of my students are finding them all of the time in all types of markets. It just takes time, persistent effort, and know-how. You'll be able to join them after reading this book.

imagine what it will sell for 15 years from now. Of course, sometimes real estate goes down, or depreciates, but over time it generally appreciates in value if you buy it at *15 to 30* percent below what it's worth today. This should protect you from a down market in most cases. Besides, if you don't want to be tied down in a market, you can wholesale and lease-option real estate and avoid most of the risk of owning while still making a profit.

Any time is a good time to get into real estate because it is always effective, producing results that can lead to great wealth.

Take Advantage of Tax Advantages

If you buy a stock, make a profit, and sell that stock, you'll likely pay a capital gains tax on that profit. People say, "I don't want to do this real estate deal because if I sell the property, I'm going to make a lot of money and pay a lot in taxes, so I'm not going to do real estate." I have a different point of view.

One of my goals is to write the IRS a check for $5 million. I love to

robert's tip

Do you like having gifts from the government? Suppose you make a good start in real estate and study all of these materials and then say, "I see how to make money in real estate; I understand all the credit finance techniques. But it's not for me. I don't want to make all that money." Congratulations, you're still going to make an incredible return on the time you invest learning about real estate investing, because if you buy your own home for even 15 percent below what it's worth—say you get a $500,000 home for $450,000—five years from now, you might be able to sell it for $700,000 and make $250,000 profit. How much tax would you likely pay on the sale of that house if it's your own home and you're married? Zero. That's because if you're married, you get a $500,000 exemption if you've owned the home for two years. In addition, you can get that exemption every two years. So every two years, you can buy your own home, sell it, make a lot of money, and likely pay no taxes.

For the last 10 years, I've owned my own homes and moved every two years. Do I think it's exciting to pack everything I own, hold a garage sale, then go to garage sales in a new city to buy more stuff that I'll sell at a garage sale two years from now? No, but I move almost every two years because it's tax-free money.

pay taxes because if I pay $5 million, that means I made $12 million and get to keep $7 million. If I send the IRS $100,000, that means I made $300,000 and kept $200,000. Real estate carries some distinct tax advantages. In many cases, you can sell real estate without paying any taxes. You can buy and sell in a self-directed individual retirement account (IRA) or do a 1031 tax-free exchange if conditions permit.

Moreover, you can write off business expenses. Let's say you've just started a business investing in real estate. You're driving your car to look for properties, talking on the phone, and maybe taking trips related to your business. All of that adds up to expenses that can be taken as tax write-offs on your income tax return. (Of course, always check with a knowledgeable accountant about write-offs in your situation.)

Owning and operating a business comes with specific tax advantages. For example, now that you're actively trying to make a profit in real estate, you can buy a computer and a copy machine for your business (plus phones, business-related gasoline for your car, etc.) and write off some or all of these expenses, too.

Exchange Rental or Investment Property

Say you've had a small apartment building or 10 houses worth $300,000 each for 15 years that you bought for $3 million. About 15 years later, the worth doubled and you can make $3 million if you sell. You'd have to pay capital gains tax—about 20 percent depending on your tax

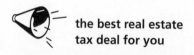

the best real estate tax deal for you

You can make up to $250,000 in tax-free profit on the sale of your own home if you are single, and you can make $500,000 if you are married and file jointly. However, you must live in the house for at least two of the past five years as your principal residence. Every two years or so, you can do the best tax-free real estate deal going.

Suppose you bought your house three years ago for $300,000 and now you sell it for $500,000. Your profit would be $200,000 because you bought it at the right price and it appreciated. That $200,000 is tax-free money to you. You can now find another good deal, live in that house for two years, and make more tax-free money when you sell it!

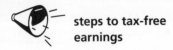

steps to tax-free earnings

Your Own Home
- Bought in 1997 for $300,000
- Retail value of $370,000
- Sold in 2003 for $570,000
- You make $570,000 – $300,000 = $270,000 tax-free profit (if you qualify)

Investment Property Using 1031 Exchange
- First investment $40,000 in 1990
- Tax-free exchange—sold for $80,000 in 1994
- Found house worth $100,000, bought it for $80,000 in 1994
- Sold house for $100,000 in 1996
- Did a 1031 tax-free exchange for a house worth $150,000, bought for $100,000
- Sold house for $250,000 cash in 1999
- Used cash as a down payment on an apartment building worth $1 million, doing a 1031 tax-free exchange; owner has not paid any taxes on these properties

bracket—on your $3 million in profit. That adds up to $600,000 in taxes, and you may have to recapture and pay taxes on some or all of the depreciation you took.

It's worthwhile getting information so you don't have to pay that, including finding out about doing a 1031 tax-free exchange. This tax exemption is available for investment property owners when you sell a property and buy a similar one for more than the amount of the first one. (The sale must take place within a certain time period.) Be sure to work with a qualified tax advisor who knows all the rules and regulations in your state. Chances are, you'll pay zero in taxes again.

To give you an example of how 1031 exchanges work, let me tell you about one of my students who bought a tiny house for $40,000 about 10 years ago, sold it for $80,000, and exchanged it into a $100,000 house. She found this $100,000 house for $80,000, then exchanged it for a $150,000 house that she purchased for $100,000. Now she's investing in apartment buildings that cost more than $1 million. She had paid zero in taxes because she kept exchanging, exchanging, and exchanging. With documentation in hand, she went to the bank or mortgage company and asked, "This apartment building is worth $1 million; would you lend us $700,000?" She borrows the funds and, again, pays zero in taxes, because, in general, borrowed funds are not taxed.

THE "YOU" FACTOR

Now that I have detailed the many advantages of investing in real estate, I have no doubt you're chomping at the bit to learn how, exactly, to find property deals, analyze them, and, ultimately, make money from them. To that I say, "Whoa, not so fast!" One important component of this effort is the "you" factor. Without you, there can be no wealth from real estate. Your wants, needs, capabilities, goals, concerns, and more all must be factored into the process. In the end, it is you who must put all that you will learn into practice. So before we talk more about real estate, we need to talk about you, which is what we do in Chapter 3.

real estate and you: the personal component of personal wealth

He who draws only on his own resources easily
comes to an end of his wealth.
—William Hazlitt

Each of you is completely different. You have different skills, different assets, different concerns, and different goals. So only you can decide what you really want to do, how much money you want to make, what you are good at and what you're not, what scares you and what does not, and what makes you comfortable and what makes you shake in your shoes. Then and only then can you start developing a plan for how you intend to go about investing in real estate. But whether you decide you are going to own 1 property or 1,000 properties, make no mistake, you are going to have a business. And every business needs a plan. Every business needs goals, and key people to achieve them.

If you start a computer company, you do not hire people who are good at raising horses. If you need sales help, you do not find people who do not like to talk to other people. Likewise, if you go into real

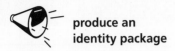

produce an identity package

People don't immediately trust other people in real estate transactions; that's one of the reasons they ask for earnest money. To develop that trust, it's a good idea to produce a professional-looking identity package. Businesses have beautiful brochures with pictures of their CEOs standing by the big corporate headquarters. Sometimes the CEO is pictured shaking hands with the mayor or other important people. Well-crafted language communicates that the corporation will help you and that it's okay to do business with them. You feel good about the company because of the impression left by its well-produced and persuasive brochure.

You, too, need a beautiful brochure. Spend some money on this; go to your copy shop and make an identity package with your name or your company's name on it. Think of a great name, such as International Real Estate Investors United. One of my company names is Superior Properties Corporation. That sounds impressive, doesn't it? It can sound big, yet have only two people in it. In fact, my young son is a shareholder in my corporation.

Your identity package should contain the following:

- A photograph of yourself
- A resume
- Letters of recommendation
- Names of associates
- Testimonials
- Photos of properties you've sold
- Signed contracts
- Documents of closings you've done
- A list of activities you enjoy

If you don't have all of these because you're new and young, then gather letters of recommendation from teachers, Boy Scout leaders, ministers, rabbis, priests, and former employers. For your list of associates, put people on the board of your company to show you work with major Realtors and mortgage companies. Of course, you must get their permission to use their names in this way.

Every time you help a Realtor or motivated seller, have that person write a testimonial for you. It might say, "Jean was a great help; she did exactly what she said she was going to do. Thank you so much, Jean, for helping me sell my house. Sincerely, Maybelle Smith, October 1999, Columbus." "Jeff was a great help; he handled the transaction very professionally."

Your list of recreational activities will serve as possible connection points.

(continued)

Continued

"Oh, you like to fly-fish? I do, too." "You like to sail, play softball, ski . . . ? Oh that's great; so do I."

Keep this folder active by adding testimonials and photos and documents of your closings. It should get bigger every month. Whenever you go to the bank or are dealing with Realtors, potential sellers, lenders, buyers—anyone in your real estate circle—show them your identity package. Whenever you see potential sellers, pull out your folder to give them evidence of your experience.

If you follow my advice and put together a beautiful identity package, you'll be in the top 5 or 10 percent of all real estate investors. It will also help you convince Realtors that you're a serious investor and serve to give you credibility.

estate investing, you want to assign yourself the jobs you are good at, the ones that inspire you.

KNOW THYSELF

Write down the real estate activities that are attractive to you, that you believe you would be good at. Maybe you love to talk to people and sell things; you will likely be good at getting tenants, putting deals together, and selling the deals. Perhaps you love detail and finance; you would be excellent at doing mortgages and financing deals, but not good at selling them. If you become irritated when people talk to you, you probably do not want to manage property.

Like Socrates said, "Know thyself." Early in my business, I learned quickly what I am not good at—accounting. I stashed receipts in shoeboxes for the first nine months of the year. The other three months, I tried to figure out what I did the first nine months. I used to balance my checkbook by calling up the bank and asking what my balance was. That is no way to run a business. I now have a service that takes care of my bookkeeping and accounting, activities that stress me out. My checkbook balances, and I know exactly where my financials are. This leaves me free to do what I love—finding and putting deals together.

What do you like to do? What is your gift? What kind of people do you like to be around? What kind of deals would fit your personality? What aspects of real estate investing fit you best? Conversely, what do

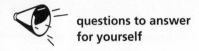

**questions to answer
for yourself**

- What is my gift?
- What do I really like to do?
- What in real estate is attractive to me?
- What do I believe I am best suited for?
- What do I absolutely *not* want to do in real estate (e.g., finding deals, putting in offers, analyzing deals, financing deals, getting partners, selling deals, managing tenants, doing repairs, bookkeeping, making cold calls, looking at properties, talking to a lot of potential buyers, talking to a lot of potential renters, talking to a lot of potential sellers, talking to investors, finding money, borrowing money, legalities, contracts, writing contracts, writing leases)?

you *not* like to do? Determine that and partner with someone who does what you hate to do.

This may sound too touchy-feely, but it is important because you do not want to buy property and then agonize because you don't like doing repairs, working with contractors, or dealing with tenants.

FORM YOUR TEAM

Whatever aspect of real estate investing you get into, you will need a team. You can build your board of directors or your team starting now. To whom will you go when you have finance questions? Legal questions? Contract or repair questions? Who will you call when you have deals to sell? Start now by asking, "Who do I want on my team?"

WRITE YOUR PLAN

When most real estate investors start out, they have one goal: to get one property. However, they have absolutely no plan. They set out to find that property and, after they buy it, they figure out what to do by accident. When tenants do not pay the rent, for example, they react quickly to evict them without researching alternatives.

Let me save you a lot of time and headache by insisting that you write a plan. A famous study about Yale graduates determined that the 3 percent

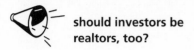

should investors be realtors, too?

What are the advantages and disadvantages of being a Realtor while being a real estate investor? Real estate investing and being a Realtor are two completely different businesses. However, if you do get your real estate license, there are advantages and some disadvantages.

You could sell property and earn a Realtor's commission, usually 6 to 7 percent of the sales price. You work in an office with access to the multiple listing service and to a computer, fax machine, and phone. You're around people who are buying and selling real estate and mortgage people, so you'll learn quickly.

But consider these disadvantages:

- Motivated sellers may not want to talk to you because they think you just want to list their house for sale if you are a Realtor.

- If anything goes wrong, you are held to a high professional standard. You may be blamed since you are a professional real estate agent operating under a lot of regulations and disclosure laws.

- There is tremendous regulation. You have to use your real estate company's contracts, disclosures, forms, and so on. In my businesses, I want as little regulation as possible.

- If you are a Realtor, you can't pay finder's fees to people who aren't Realtors, so when your repair person or postal carrier brings you the deal of the century and wants a finder's fee, you can't pay it. If you pay finder's fees to other Realtors, they will probably stop working for you if you don't pay them.

- It requires paying a lot of fees: monthly fees, access fees, license fees, education fees.

I gave up my real estate license because there were too many rules. Even though I wanted to follow them, I wasn't sure I was always in compliance because they were complicated. For instance, every time I talked to someone, I had to tell that person immediately that I was a Realtor. If I ran an ad, I had to put the Realtor's symbol in the ad or I'd be violating the rules. If I placed a For Rent sign on my own property, I'd have to put "Realtor" on the sign. There are so many rules and regulations, I decided to give it up.

Instead, I became part owner of a real estate brokerage. I wasn't a Realtor, but I did own part of the company, and when people made commissions I received part of them. You can own a brokerage and walk in the office and ask someone there to run the comps. Realtors can prove to be a big asset to investors, but they represent two completely different businesses. You must weigh the advantages and disadvantages of being a Realtor and/or being an investor.

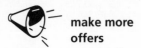

make more offers

A gentleman named Hal lives in my town, owns a lot more property, and makes a lot more money than I do. Another gentleman named John in Ohio owns more than 900 properties, and he makes a lot more money than Hal. Why is this? Here is the secret: Hal makes more offers than I do, and John makes more offers than Hal. If you never make an offer on a property, you will never get one. I promise that if you make enough offers, some of them—not all of them—will be accepted. Therefore, if you are not happy with how much property or income you are generating from your real estate business, the solution is simple: Make more offers.

of those graduates who wrote down their goals for the future financially outperformed the other 97 percent three to five times.

I challenge you to, in the next 48 hours, sit down with your loved ones and write out your goals. Decide what you want to have for your 30-day plan, followed by your 60- and 90-day plans, your 6-month plan, and your 1-, 5-, 10-, and 20-year plans. Schedule a couple of hours to record these goals and structure your plans. Remember, your plan does not have to be very long—I suggest between two and six pages. It should include the following items:

- How much property you want to have (in each time frame)
- What type of activities you want to be involved in
- How much money you want to make (in each time frame)
- How much net worth you want to develop

Most important, write down how you will reach each of your goals—your plan of action. How many phone calls will you make? How many properties will you look at? It is one thing to say, "I would like $10 million worth of real estate," but it means nothing if you do not say how you will get there.

PLAN YOUR PERFECT DAY AT WORK

Tie your goals into creating a perfect day at work. How would your perfect day go? Would you have a big office, or a little one? Would you work out of your home? Where would it be located—in a city, on the beach, or in the mountains?

Beyond the physical setup, determine the nature of your business. What kind of deals would you make? What would your portfolio look like? How much money could you make that day? What would you do to bring in money? Who would you work with?

I planned my perfect day at work a few years ago in Nashville, Tennessee. I saw myself by the beach. I would wake up and exercise, ride around, take some phone calls, do some deals, have lunch, rest in the afternoon or go to the swimming pool, check my messages, do more work in the afternoon, put some deals together, and go out at night or spend time with my family and friends. I would also travel a lot.

I made that plan when I lived in a half-room office in Nashville. Today, I live in a beautiful condominium apartment overlooking downtown Miami and the beach. I ride my scooter and my bicycle around. I wake up early to work out or do yoga on the beach. I come home, check messages, make some phone calls, listen to a few angry tenant requests on voice mail, go to lunch, work some in the afternoon, hang out, and travel a lot. Most of my days are just as I pictured.

PLAN YOUR PERFECT DAY AT PLAY

Besides your real estate goals, be sure to make overall financial goals, personal goals, family goals, and spiritual goals. How much vacation do you want to have? How much time do you want to spend with your loved ones? How do you want to relax?

When you know this, you can plan your perfect day of play. Write down what that perfect day looks like. Where are you going to be? What are you doing? Who are you with? When you make that first wholesale deal or do a lease option or buy, fix up, and sell a property, reward yourself. Take a small percentage of your profit and get that perfect day of play under way. Maybe you want to take a balloon ride, go on a picnic, go to the mountains, go to the beach, or go on a cruise ship—whatever it is, first set your goals by writing them down.

If you do not have the energy to write down your goals, I can assure you that you won't have the energy to make your real estate deals happen.

Let me give you an example. At a workshop, one of the participants came up to me and said, "Robert, I am going to learn this stuff. All I want to do is make $6,000 and pay off my credit card bill. That is my goal." He went out, flipped one property, earned $6,200, and paid off his Visa bill. He met his goal. He was thrilled.

Another student said, "Robert, I have a lot of overhead. I used to be a corporate executive making a lot of money. I need to make $20,000 a month, no less." He wrote that down as his goal. To make that amount, we agreed that he would have to do a couple of flips a month, buy rental property, broker mortgages, and get active. He really likes doing these activities and now makes between $20,000 and $30,000 a month, just as he pictured.

KNOW WHAT YOU'RE WORTH

My parents, who brought me up well, always said, "Do not ever talk about money, sex, religion, or credit." I love to talk about all of these things because I find them fascinating; most people do not. However, if you are going to be a successful real estate investor with various income sources, you *do* need to talk about money and credit. You need to get them under control, or at least get started on them. Most real estate investors who have been supersuccessful have also been superbroke.

Start by taking a financial snapshot of where you are today. How much cash do you have? How much credit? What is your credit score? Requesting a copy of your credit report and obtaining a financial statement from a bank or mortgage company will help you to determine what you want to do with your real estate investing as you put these activities into practice. Six months or a year from now, you can compare your snapshot then with now. Realize that you have to know where you are today to be able to get to where you want to be tomorrow.

If you take time now to answer the following questions, you will have a much better idea of what you want to get into. In addition, you will avoid a lot of headaches and frustrations that most investors never take the time to think about.

- How much can you borrow (if you need to) to make real estate investments?
- How much access to cash do you have?

 **think about it**

Some people spend most of their time thinking about what they *can't* do or what won't work. Some people, perhaps you, think about how they *can* do something. In my early years of investing, most people told me I couldn't buy any property or own my first duplex because I had no credit. Instead of listening to them, I found a cosigner who had great credit to partner with. I found the deals and my cosigner signed the loans with me so I could borrow the money I needed. Word of caution: Make sure you've found a *good deal* before you commit your credit or especially someone else's credit to a real estate deal. What have you accomplished in the past that people told you that you could not? How did it feel when you accomplished it?

- What are your assets?
- What do you own? (Houses? Cars? Investments?)
- What are your liabilities?
- What are your debts? (Mortgages? Credit cards?)
- How much is your life insurance? Your retirement account?

Take the next two days, the next 48 hours, to make a plan. Decide where you are and where you want to be. Write down your goals and share them with others. You are on your way to developing numerous sources of real estate income. (We'll talk more about your credit in Chapter 12.)

DON'T DO IT ALONE

Perhaps all this talk about your personal commitment, your money, and your credit situation has made you nervous. But relax; don't, as I did when I first started, begin to overanalyze, doubt, and worry. Even if you don't have a lot of money, and your credit is not great, I promise you, you can succeed in real estate. And, as I explain in this section, you don't have to do it alone. You can rely on other people's ideas, time, money, and credit. Really.

Use Other People's Ideas

You do not have to create or reinvent successful real estate investing. You're better off finding other successful people who've learned what you want to know and using their ideas. That's why you have coaches and mentors. It's called other people's ideas (OPI). In 2003, I spent about $50,000 consulting with successful investors and learning just a few of the things they do. I'm using their ideas instead of trying to reinvent everything. Even though I am a successful investor, I am always trying to learn from others and improve.

Other successful businesses do that, too. Bill Gates didn't write the operating systems for Microsoft. He went to IBM and said, "If we had this operating system I envision, what would you pay for it?" When the decision makers showed interest, he wrote a contract for them to buy the yet-to-be-created operating system for about $1 million plus a few dollars for every computer that used it. What he did was controversial. In fact, three of his partners walked out of the meeting and told Bill he was crazy. But, really, he was smart. He did what's called a wholesale/flip— he found the buyer before he found the product. Then he went back to his home in Seattle, found a programmer, and paid the programmer about $50,000 to write the operating system. Then he took that contract and wholesaled the information to IBM—and others. He used OPI to great effect.

Use Other People's Time

How many deals can you look at in a week? How much bookkeeping can you do? How many properties can you fix? How many buyers can you find? How many deals can you fund?

Let's face it, you're limited by time. But you can get other people to use their time. For example, I have about 40 people looking for deals for me right now. (It should be 100, but I'm lazy sometimes.) Instead of looking for deals by yourself, instead of doing your own bookkeeping and financing, use other people's time.

Use Other People's Money and Credit

You have a choice: When you start your real estate investing business, you can use all of your own money and all of your own credit to buy

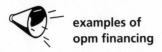

examples of opm financing

Mr. R. in Florida says his entire family works in real estate. He himself owns hundreds of beautiful properties. However, Mr. R.'s name is not on any deeds, and he does not have any liability, because he has partners and investors (e.g., doctors, lawyers, accountants, bankers) whose names are on the deeds. He discloses every agreement in writing. He does not owe a cent to anyone. When he sells his houses, he earns from $20,000 up to $100,000, and the investors get their money back plus one-half of the profits.

I know a full-time student who makes between $80,000 and $120,000 a year as a part-time real estate investor. He digs up a good deal, puts a property under contract, finds investors, buys the property with their money, fixes it up, then sells it for a profit anywhere in the range of $5,000 to $12,000.

---

properties. However, the most successful investors in the United States, those who own lots of property and make 10 times more money than other investors, never use *one penny* of their own money or *one point* of their own credit.

I recommend using other people's money (OPM) and other people's credit (OPC) because you can reduce your risk to almost zero.

Funding Partners

When you do any business, know what you're good at, what you have, and what you do not have. Then you can find others who have what you don't have. For instance, I can't type so I don't try to type; I find a typist whom I pay to type for me. Similarly, if you don't have any money or credit, find people who do. They need what you have: the energy, the time, and the information to find good deals.

Bill Gates certainly didn't fund all the start-up costs of Microsoft. He asked seven people to lend him about $50,000 each to get his company up and running. Some of them told him, "This computer stuff won't work." However, five of them kicked in $50,000 each. Now some of them are on the list of the 100 richest people in the world, according to *Forbes* magazine.

You can do the same by forming a limited liability company (LLC) with others interested in investing. They could be uncles, aunts, wealthy friends, attorneys, accountants, employers, retirees—select people you trust and want to work with. You could find the deals and do the legwork; they could fund the deals and benefit from the tax advantages available through real estate. (As you set up your partnership, be sure to claim at least 51 percent ownership—even 70 or 80 percent—so you can keep the majority of control needed.)

A successful investor I know in Florida owns 300 houses. He either puts them in an LLC or in the name of his partners—those who borrowed the money to buy these houses. This investor owns 60 percent of the properties. He makes all the decisions about managing them and when to sell them. This arrangement allows his partners to build their wealth as the tenants pay off the debt or the houses. Each month there is positive cash flow, and when the houses are sold, everyone profits.

Here is how he does it. Using many of the techniques in this book for finding deals, negotiating, and so on, he locates a likely property. For instance, he found a house in Florida worth $150,000. It needed $10,000 in repairs, and he negotiated a price of $99,000 because the seller was motivated. With repairs, he needed $109,000 to buy the house worth $150,000. He joined forces with a wealthy businessman who had just lost a lot of money in the stock market and wanted to get into real estate. The wealthy businessman was easily able to borrow $120,000 on the $150,000 house, because he had great credit and excellent banking connections. The house is titled to a limited liability company (LLC), with my friend owning 60 percent and the wealthy borrower owning 40 percent. All of the agreements and disclosures are in writing.

My friend received $5,000 up front for finding the deal. The excess $6,000 (they had borrowed $120,000, but needed only $109,000, minus the $5,000) went into a resource account for any expenses. They lease-optioned the house for $1,400 a month. The note, taxes, and insurance were about $1,000 a month. The wealthy borrower gets most of the depreciation of the house as a write-off against his taxable income. Each month these partners split the cash flow after the expenses are paid 60-40.

Use Common Sense

In conclusion to this discussion, I must remind you to take your time to find people who behave ethically. Using other people's ideas, time, money, and credit does not absolve you of the responsibility to use common sense and be duly diligent whenever you involve other people in your real estate dealings.

At this juncture, I've explained how to get started right, detailed how and why real estate is such a great wealth builder, and introduced "you" into the process. Now it's time to look at some properties. In the next chapter, I'll define the various types of real estate and their advantages and disadvantages when it comes to investing.

chapter 4

all types of real estate: advantages and disadvantages

To win without risk is to triumph without glory.
—Pierre Corneille, *Le Cid*, 1636

New real estate investors always ask me what type of real estate is best: land, houses, duplexes, and so on. Should they get into high-end property? Low-end property? Middle-income property? Commercial property? Apartment buildings?

My advice is to pursue whatever you are interested in. Do not ever listen to someone who says, "Only do this type of real estate. Only get into houses. Never do commercial. Only do commercial. Do not do houses. Big apartment buildings are better than little apartment buildings. Trailer parks are the best, better than houses." The truth is, it all can work.

Your job is to find a good deal in real estate, whether it is a $3,000 trailer, a $30,000 house, a $300,000 luxury home, a $3 million apartment building, or a $30 million commercial property. Find properties you are comfortable and familiar with at first, then expand. This chapter gives you an overview of different types of investing, so you can consider the advantages and disadvantages of getting into them.

RENTAL PROPERTY

Rentals can be an excellent wealth builder. You buy and hold properties, pay off the debt, and watch the value appreciate. Rentals give you some tax advantages, too. Here are some of your choices.

Trailers and Weekly Rentals

I know some people who will not rent anything if they cannot wheel it around. When I got started in real estate, I would buy a house or duplex for $50,000 in Tennessee and rent it for maybe $700 or $800 a month, at the same time paying off a note of $400 or $500 a month. I was making $200 to $400 every month. For $4,000, my friends would buy a trailer that was 10 or 15 years old. They would fix it up and rent it for $100 or $150 a week. They recovered their initial investment in eight months or less and earned $500 or $600 a month in rent after that. In these two examples, which deal is better? The last one is . . . on paper. However, as with anything, there are advantages and disadvantages.

Advantages

- The cash flow is great.
- The amount you have to invest to get started is minimal.
- The return that you get on your cash flow is good.

Disadvantages

- You deal with a lot of management hassles, transitions, and turnovers.
- You will spend money to keep the cash coming in.

Analyze the situation well, and make sure you count your time and money so you can make a good return on your investment.

Single-Family Homes

What about basic, single-family bread-and-butter homes rented to low- and moderate-income families? You do not need to have a lot of money to get into them; you can leverage out of them; you can buy them for less than what they are worth. They are in high demand, so they are fairly easy to rent and sell if you take care of them.

Advantages

- They are easy to rent.
- They are easy to sell.
- They appreciate fairly nicely.

Disadvantages

- If you own a little house here and a little house there on scattered sites, they are management-intensive.
- If your tenants are low- and moderate-income (or at any level of income) and you do not screen them well, you may face plenty of repairs when they move out.

Condominiums

Renting condominiums has advantages and disadvantages, too.

Advantages

- Condominiums are fairly easy to rent. Sometimes they are easy to sell, but not as easy as single-family homes.
- Condominium owners are only responsible for the interior; common areas are kept up by the management association.

Disadvantages

- Condominiums have maintenance and management fees that range from $60 to $300 a month to cover insurance and upkeep of common areas. These sometimes eat into your cash flow.
- The condo association needs to be well funded and not facing any big expenses like a new roof or parking lot. Always do your research first.

Duplexes, Triplexes, and Quadruplexes

Here are some pros and cons of renting duplexes, triplexes, and quadruplexes.

Advantages

- They are easy to finance most of the time because they are deemed residential real estate. This means that anything with fewer than four units can be financed through a residential loan, so they are easier to finance. Remember, properties that are easy to finance are easy to buy and sell.

- They have more than one unit bringing in rent, which helps the cash flow.

- They are fairly easy to rent because people would rather live with just 1 or 2 neighbors than with 400 in a large apartment building.

Disadvantages

- They are harder to sell than houses in a slow market. Single-family, three-bedroom homes are the easiest group to sell.

- They are harder to finance than single-family homes.

- Their biggest disadvantage is also one of their advantages: Because more people are paying rent, collecting rent becomes complicated. Rent-paying situations create more turnover, more repairs, more phone calls, and more management headaches.

Small Apartment Buildings

Smaller apartment buildings, containing between 5 and 100 units, are part of a fragmented market. A lot of mom-and-pop owner-operators run small apartment buildings.

Advantages

- You receive great cash flow.

- You can usually hire an on-site manager to take care of things because all of the tenants live in one place and are not scattered.

- You can have economies of scale because all of the apartments are in one place.

Disadvantages

- As the number of units goes up, vacancy and repair rates go up, which translates into more turnover, more repairs, more people, and more headaches.

- It is harder to sell an apartment building than a home if the market goes bad because it is an investment property.
- It is more difficult to find financing for an apartment building than for a home. Rarely will a bank or mortgage company loan more than between 60 and 80 percent of the purchase price of a small apartment building.

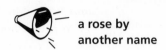

a rose by another name

In certain areas of the United States, duplexes are called *doubles,* triplexes are called *triples,* and quadruplexes are called *fourplexes.* In my opinion, it doesn't matter what you call them if they make money for you.

Large Apartment Buildings

Large apartment complexes are usually run by large organizations. This market requires a lot of capital and can be very competitive.

Advantages

- Large apartment buildings provide economies of scale.
- Large apartment buildings are easy to manage with all tenants in one place. Finding great deals on apartment buildings becomes more competitive with 100- to 200-unit complexes because many large commercial companies invest in these. Then you may be competing against large real estate companies and institutions with tremendous amounts of capital. However, many real estate investors profit well from the smaller complexes that have from 10 to 50 units.

Disadvantages

- They can be hard to finance because of size.
- They can be tough to sell in a down market.

COMMERCIAL PROPERTY

Commercial property here refers to strip centers, office buildings, and commercial warehouses.

Advantages

- The tenants generally take care of all the repairs, unlike in residential properties.
- The rents can be lucrative, especially for big spaces.

Disadvantages

- Commercial property is more difficult to finance than residential property.
- Commercial property often requires time to find another tenant that suits the space. This means that you have to be willing to pay the note or pay the costs, taxes, and insurance while the space becomes rented and retooled for a new tenant.
- Commercial property stays empty longer than residential property when the economy is down.

LAND DEVELOPMENTS

Land developments involve investors finding land, getting it under control, improving it with roads or utilities, then selling it for a big profit, either through a residential developer or a commercial developer. It is a great business.

> One of my favorite sayings: "The two best businesses in the world are buying whiskey by the bottle and selling it by the shot, and buying land by the acre and selling it by the lot."

Advantages

- A land development gives you the potential for a tremendous profit because you are dealing with a bigger chunk of land.
- A land development will likely increase in value, especially if you improve it with roads and services.

Disadvantages

- You have to have *real* money because the land does not produce any income.
- You have costs (e.g., mortgage, taxes, insurance) while you are holding the land.

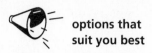

**options that
suit you best**

Your main job in developing unlimited riches in real estate is to find good deals. Once you learn the tools (e.g., for wholesaling and lease optioning described in Chapters 7 and 8, respectively), it does not matter whether the property is a piece of land, a house, a duplex, or a giant apartment building. Use the methods in this book to learn which options suit you best.

- You can sell land easily in prosperous times; however, in hard times, you may have difficulty selling it.

TIME TO ACT

This chapter concludes Part I of the book. These four chapters have laid the knowledge foundation on which you will begin to develop your eventual expertise as a real estate investor. In Part II, you will learn how to become a deal "architect." I explain how to find deals, find motivated sellers, and the ins and outs of two of the best ways to make a profit in real estate: by wholesaling and lease optioning.

part II

properties and profits

chapter 5

finding great deals

*Patience, persistence and perspiration make an unbeatable
combination for success.*

—Napolean Hill

This part explains how to analyze deals; contract deals; lease-option
deals; wholesale property; buy, fix up, and sell property; rent property;
and determine many other possible avenues of income you can get from
real estate investing. But first you must understand how to find a good
deal.

If you cannot find a good deal in real estate, you cannot make any
money. You cannot develop all of those sources of income without finding good deals.

WHAT IS A GREAT DEAL?

Let's say a friend of yours is getting divorced, has to move away, needs
cash quickly, and says, "I have this Jaguar worth about $50,000. It's in
great shape. If I could just get $30,000 for it, I'd be okay." The car was
brand new the year before, purchased for about $55,000.

Could you figure out a way to make money off that Jaguar? You could
call dealers, who are wholesalers, and ask, "What is a 2001 Jaguar worth
today?" They might reply, "About $50,000." So you would ask, "What

would you pay for it?" and they might say, "We'd have to make something on the resale, so we'd pay $42,000 for it."

If the dealership gave you $42,000 and you gave your friend $30,000, you would make $12,000. Alternatively, you could run an ad in the newspaper offering the Jaguar for, say, $45,000. You would make even more money. Or you could take $30,000 from your savings or borrow from a bank, lease the Jaguar for $600 a month, and bring in money every month for it.

You have these choices in real estate, too, but first you have to find a good deal like your friend with the Jaguar handed you. If you find a good deal, you will make good money. If you find a great deal, you will make great money.

FINDING MOTIVATED SELLERS

To find good deals, find motivated sellers. If a property is worth $100,000 in the marketplace and the seller wants $99,000 for it, the seller simply is not hungry to sell. What motivates some people to sell at below-market prices, and how can you identify them?

When people are selling a house and are eager to get rid of it, the only thing they care about is solving their problem. You may think they care most about the money involved. That's simply not true. You may think they want to sell a house. That's not true, either. This goes back to the most important question: Why do people buy a home? To spend a lot of money? No. Because it's good to buy a home? No. It's important to understand *why* people buy homes; then you'll understand why they *sell* them, and then you'll also know how to negotiate with potential motivated sellers.

Owning a home involves paying off a mortgage and spending money for taxes, insurance, and repairs. Many people could rent something for a lot less and live in a nice place with everything taken care of. But they buy homes based on their need for security and status, which is why some people live in houses that are too big and expensive for them. They also buy houses to get into better school districts for their children. But mostly, their decision has to do with emotion, not rationalization.

People also *sell* homes for emotional reasons. They either have a problem or they're avoiding problems. They have "pain" they want to "fix." They're getting divorced; they're getting remarried; they have to

robert's tip

One day, I called someone who wanted $480,000 for several houses. He said he had to have cash. The only thing on his mind was a $5,000 debt that had come due; he didn't have $5,000 to pay it, and the pain of the creditors calling him to pay his debt was becoming intense. He wanted to get rid of this debt. In addition, he didn't want the hassle, obligation, responsibility, and liability of managing the houses he'd inherited. He thought he wanted $480,000. He really wanted only $5,000. On the rest, $475,000, he took owner's terms. You have to find out what someone's real need or problem is.

It doesn't matter what your profession—people don't care whether you're a doctor, a lawyer, a real estate agent, an investor, an alien, or an illegal immigrant. They care about fixing their problems. As an investor, I'm rarely asked who I am or what my title or my job is. People don't care, and I usually don't tell them. Offer only the information they need and stay focused on solving their problem.

move out of the city or state; they're starting a new job. Sometimes, they have to sell their homes quickly. They may have to pay off the mortgage to have money to buy another home. Or they're in over their heads financially.

Your job as a real estate investor is to discover their problem and solve it.

Loss of job. Financial problems. Estate sale. Job transfer. Illness and no health insurance. Recent divorce or remarriage. Overextended credit, tax problems, tired landlords. These events can all lead to motivated sellers. Here's an example of what happens.

A homeowner has $400,000 in debt and the bank is demanding payment; the house may be worth $555,000, but the homeowner may not be able to get the money to pay off that debt or stop foreclosure. It's possible the home will be foreclosed and the owner's credit wrecked. You can help turn this into a win-win situation.

Perhaps all the sellers really want is to get $5,000 cash to pay off the bank and move. If not, they could be foreclosed upon and end up in real trouble. You could help the seller and the bank by putting the house under contract for $405,000—$5,000 to the seller and $400,000 to pay

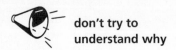

don't try to understand why

If you follow this advice, you will save a lot of time, headaches, and psychic energy in real estate investing:

Stop trying to figure out why people do what they do.

Why do people smoke? They know it is going to kill them. Why do people not go to the gym? Why do they not take care of their health? Why do they not donate money to charity? Why isn't everybody happy? Why do people spend ridiculous amounts of money on ridiculous things?

This book is not about teaching psychology. If you are reading it, you want to be a successful real estate investor, not a counselor. Your job is to find good deals, not to understand why people do what they do. However, it is wise to find out the circumstances people face. Their life events certainly affect their motivation to sell at below-market pricing.

off the loan. Contact your network of buyers, investors, and real estate agents; perhaps you could find a buyer who would pay $455,000 for the $550,000 house. If it is a good deal, the buyers will come. At closing, the bank has its loan paid off, the sellers have been saved from foreclosure and have $5,000 to move, the end buyer gets a great deal, and you earn $55,000 (less any closing costs you had to pay) for finding a good deal and putting a buyer and seller together.

I am not suggesting that you take advantage or rip people off. If you ever have a transaction in which every party is not completely satisfied with the deal, move on.

You can experiment with a variety of ways to find sellers, including going through newspapers and brokers. Be sure to use these approaches consistently so you know which ones work best for you.

READING NEWSPAPER ADS

I got started in this business Sunday mornings while enjoying my favorite hot drink at home and reading the newspaper. About half of all the deals I have ever found, even the great ones, have come from newspaper ads. Calling on ads at least every Sunday or more often will get you started. If you follow sports, you read the Sunday paper religiously. You learn about the heights and weights of the athletes, their playing statistics, even their arrest records in some cases. If you study the real estate section in the same way, you will become an expert in real estate like you are in sports. It is similar to how some people follow stocks. They know every detail about them and watch their movements 15 times a day. If you did one-tenth of that activity in real estate by steadily going to the real estate section every week, you would become an expert in real estate.

When you read the newspaper, what are you looking for? Suspects—highly motivated sellers who become prospects. The following nine ideas suggest where to look to get started.

For Rent Ads

If a property is for rent, it is often empty and the owners have a mortgage on it but are not collecting rent. The landlord or management company may be tired of renting it out and keeping it repaired. Sometimes you can get some great deals and help the owner get out of the business altogether.

For Sale by Owner Ads

If people are selling their houses by themselves, that might mean they cannot afford a Realtor, do not want to get a Realtor, or are in a hurry to sell.

"must sell"

A student of mine, Don, saw a "Must Sell" ad in the newspaper for a commercial property in Miami, Florida. He did not know much about Miami, but he called the broker listed in the ad and asked this critical question: "Why are you selling?" The broker replied, "The woman is selling because her husband was the landlord. He just passed away and she doesn't want to manage it. She's tired of it. She wants to dump it. The building is worth as much as $1.4 million but it needs $200,000 of work. She'd take $500,000 for it." Don offered a lot less than that and got the building under contract for $290,000. He wants to wholesale it and stands to make between $100,000 and $300,000. The end buyer will also get a great deal because Don is asking $700,000 to $800,000 for this $1.4 million building.

Who wins? Everybody. The widow is happy to let go of the property after making money with it over the last 30 years. The broker will make a good commission; Don will see a large profit; the end buyer will get an incredible deal. And it all started from answering an ad in the local newspaper.

For Sale Ads

Look at For Sale ads to quickly learn what property sells for in specific neighborhoods. Search for phrases such as "Must Sell," "Make Offer," and "Won't Last." I circle those ads and call to find suspects who might become prospects.

In the process of calling, you will learn which Realtors are active in those areas. Get to know them because if you ever find a deal in their territory, they could help you locate buyers or sellers.

Investment Property Ads

I like to respond to ads under the heading "Investment Properties" because I know investors own these properties being advertised. An investor or landlord has either purchased a property years ago and wants the profits from the appreciation in value, or has bought a bad deal and is tired of messing with the property. In both cases, the owner could be highly motivated to sell.

When I call, I always ask, "Do you have or know of any other properties for sale?" I recommend always asking that question when you call. Here is why.

I once responded to an ad from this section and the older gentleman who answered said, "I've got this property and I'm selling it at 30 percent below what it's worth. I'll do owner's terms. I have pictures of it and I really want to sell, so I'll be more than glad to work with you." Then I asked that important question. "Do you have any others?" He said, "I'm so glad you asked. I've got 88 more, all with pictures and documentation." I ended up buying all of them and flipped about 50 in about a year.

Lease-Option Ads

Check for a Lease-Option section in your paper. Investors looking for deals or putting deals together usually place ads here. Remember, they are investors. And if you are also an investor who is going to be wholesaling, you not only want deals that you can buy but you want people you can sell to. Always get their names, addresses, phone numbers, fax numbers, e-mail addresses, and what type of property they like. Another critical question to ask is: "Do you know of any good sources of financing?" Build your lists of people who can get you money as well as get you deals.

Every time you talk to an investor, you are looking for three things:

1. A deal *you* can buy
2. A deal of yours that *they* can buy
3. Good sources of financing

Auction Ads

Auctions, listed in the back of the real estate section, are becoming a popular way to sell property. Some estimate that in the next five years, about 40 to 50 percent of all property may be auctioned.

Auction companies advertise, conduct the auction, sell the property, and close the deal 10 to 30 days later. If they have deals they cannot auction, they sell them at a discount because auctioneers are always finding motivated sellers who want to off-load their properties quickly.

When you go to real estate auctions, whom do you meet? Buyers who have cash. (Some deals offer owner's terms or financing, but many require cash.) So go to an auction as if it were a cocktail party. Meet everybody there and build your list of buyers. Get names, addresses, phone numbers, e-mail addresses, and fax numbers. These investors find deals that they could pass on to you, and vice versa. All the while, you keep your eyes open for a great deal.

Legal Notices

You will find legal notices in many newspapers. They announce bankruptcies, divorces, foreclosures, and estate sales. You might find highly motivated sellers in any one of these areas, plus you can find a lot of great deals and work with your attorney on the technical details. These deals can be worth the effort.

Every major city has a legal newspaper. Call a local attorney or go to a magazine shop, find out the name, and buy it. It is full of foreclosures, tax liens, bankruptcies, estate sales, and divorces. You do not have to understand the legal mumbo jumbo. You simply call the attorney listed or get an address off the legal notice and send a letter asking about suspects for good deals.

Obituaries

If an obituary is in the newspaper, what does that mean to you? The deceased usually leaves behind real estate, furniture, cars, and often family members who live all over. You could be doing their relatives a service by writing or calling them and saying, "I am so sorry to hear about your loss, but if you have any property you want to dispose of quickly, I can help you. I might be interested in taking it over." In a lot of instances, people say, "We don't want to mess with this house. The children and cousins have moved across the country. Just take the house; you're doing us a favor. Yes, we know we're selling way below what it is worth, but we don't have time to deal with it. Too many memories. Just take it."

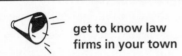

get to know law firms in your town

Generally, in any given town, a couple of top law firms handle most of the foreclosures and bankruptcies. Get to know the people in those firms and work with them. Understand that they care about client confidentiality, so they cannot tell you certain things, but they do know about pending deals. They will call somebody about them, so it might as well be you.

I have been teaching this method for years and one of my students has been extremely successful. He responds to all the obituaries in writing and usually gets about 10 to 20 deals a year in a very small town. Many times, the people write him a letter thanking him after he has put the property under contract, flipped it, fixed it up, and sold it. They say, "Thank you so much for taking that property off our hands. We didn't want to have to deal with everything." So sometimes he not only gets the houses, but also acquires cars, furniture, and collectibles.

Neighborhood Newspapers

Some of the best deals can be found in the *Thrifty Nickel*, the *Shopper's News*, and other neighborhood papers because people who place ads there cannot afford to advertise in the big paper. I have experimented and found that if you have $200 to advertise with, you will likely get better results from advertising in the smaller papers. Not only are they good sources for finding deals, but you also get more bang for your buck in advertising. (More about advertising later in this chapter.)

DRIVING FOR DOLLARS

Driving for dollars. Doesn't it sound like a game show? "Good evening, ladies and gentlemen. In tonight's edition of *Driving for Dollars*, we have two contestants." But you can make a lot of money at this game, which is my favorite way of finding good deals. It is fun to go with someone who will write down the addresses as you find promising properties.

Pick a neighborhood that you are interested in: one that is in transition, is being fixed up, has houses that need work, and so on. Drive around it slowly and try to find at least 20 addresses you can write down for neglected, vacant, or condemned homes, ones with signs saying For Sale, For Sale by Owner, or For Rent.

Be persistent. You may have to call and call and call to find the owners. Start by calling the Registrar of Deeds, getting on the Internet, and going to the local tax records office to locate the owners. Ask a Realtor friend to look them up on the MLS computer. Then call or write to the owners once you find them.

As you drive around, how do you tell if a house might be owned by a motivated seller? Look for the following characteristics.

Neglect

Needy homes have gutters hanging loose, roofs with holes in them, and horrible-looking yards with trash lying everywhere. A general rule in real estate is this: The worse the disrepair, the better the deal. As an investor, begin to love houses that have black goo dripping out of the ceiling, animal dung on the carpet, holes in the wall, broken windows, and 14 feet of garbage in the yard. The more work the house needs, the more motivated the seller will be. The more motivated the seller, the better the deal will be.

The best deal my friend John ever got involved a house that had 35 feet of garbage in the front yard. Drug addicts had lived in it. When he walked into the house, he could not even get access to the basement because of the garbage.

But the real estate market was hot in this neighborhood and 50 people looked at the house during its first two days on the market. Everybody who saw it walked away in disgust. Most people insist on buying a house that looks like a new present with a bow on it.

So John went into the trashed-out house, took a big breath in the smelly environment, and declared, "Ah, Paradise. Eureka. The mother lode." He figured that house was worth about $350,000 fixed up. He determined it needed about $50,000 of repairs. So he put it under contract for $140,000 (less than half of its value) and got the deal done. This example proves my point: The worse the house, the better the deal.

Undeveloped Land

My friend Bill, an investor in Nashville, Tennessee, finds big chunks of land—20 acres, 50 acres, 200 acres—negotiates the price, and puts the land under contract. I asked Bill, "Where do you find most of these deals?" He said, "I drive around, find land on the edge of town, and either talk to the neighbors or write a letter and find the owner. I have never used a Realtor because the property is rarely listed."

Bill finds owners, asks if they would like to sell their land, and gets an option to buy it. If it is unimproved farmland, he reads the property codes for that area and often gets the land rezoned to make it more attractive to future buyers. He might borrow money from a partner or from the bank, then puts in roads and utilities to increase the land's value immediately. Three months to two years later, he sells this land (under option at $800,000) for $1.5 million to $3 million. You can do that, too.

Vacant Homes

If houses are empty, the grass is high, the bushes are overgrown, and the properties look deserted, could those sellers be motivated? Absolutely. Put them on your list of suspects.

Condemned Homes

Look for that yellow tape that says, "Unfit for human habitation." This signifies a code violation. That is exciting for investors because owners who have already been to court might be highly motivated to sell. The codes enforcement area of the Housing Administration has fined them. The fines are equivalent to saying, "If you do not fix this house, we will fine you more, and if you still don't fix it by a certain time, we will bull-doze your property."

Some condemned homes require a tremendous amount of work to fix up, maybe too much. The windows could be broken and the electricity or the heat may not work. You always have to ask if it is a good investment.

Not only can you spot these "diamonds in the rough" while driving for dollars, you can access a list of addresses for condemned homes posted by the Housing Administration.

For Rent Signs

If a house is for rent, you might locate a highly motivated landlord who bought the property 20 years ago for one-fifth of what it is worth today and is tired of it. The best ones are the empty ones. Call about these, too.

For Sale and For Sale by Owner Signs

As you drive for dollars, look for For Sale and For Sale by Owner signs. Some of these signs might say, "Make Offer," so pay close attention. Because you are still driving neighborhoods, learning about the neighborhoods, and getting suspects, make a point of meeting the Realtors and brokers who are active in that area. You will learn a tremendous amount from talking with them and from carefully reading the signs.

Auctions

In addition to the auctions listed in the newspaper, look for other auction companies in the Yellow Pages. When you drive around for dollars, you

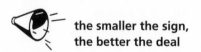

the smaller the sign, the better the deal

Mary, a student of mine, was once driving around (you have to go really slow when you are driving for dollars) and almost missed a little bitty sign behind a bush. She got out of her car, jumped over a low fence, moved the bush, and saw one of those little For Sale signs available for 90 cents at the hardware store. She could hardly even read the phone number. In fact, she wrote down eight different phone numbers she thought it might be, and found the seventh one to be correct. On the phone call, she asked the man who answered, "How long has your house been for sale?" He replied, "Six months. You're the first caller." How would you like to be a market of one? Mary bought that house for about half of what it was worth, wholesaled it, and made about $20,000.

She also asked that magic question, "Do you have any others?" He replied, "Yes, I have another one. It's a few blocks away. No one has called about that one, either." She drove by that house and saw the sign there had completely fallen off. She was able to make a good deal on that house, too.

will see signs about upcoming auctions. Call all of the auction companies and *get on their announcement lists,* so whenever they do an auction, they send you a notice for auctions of a commercial property, house, apartment building, land, and so on. Attend all of those auctions that have properties; you might find a great deal.

Locating Owners

What if you can't find owners? One investor was driving for dollars and found some vacant homes, wrote the addresses down, went to the Internet, and looked on the tax rolls, but still could not find the owners.

It is almost always certain that *someone* owns a property, whether it is an individual, a corporation, or an estate. There is a name on a title at the tax records office; it might even belong to someone who died 10 years ago. Or it might have been a factor in some kind of lawsuit. To find out what happened to the title, hire a title searcher to get the names of people listed, then locate them.

You could also hire a private investigator. For between $100 and $500, private investigators can find owners and probably learn what happened to the property. (My web site, www.shemin.com, gives names of private investigators we recommend.)

Now, what if no one owns that property and no title exists? Then you go to court, hire an attorney, and file an action to "quiet title." A judge will decide what is necessary to clear up the title or get a good title. Sometimes the judge will ask you or your attorney to advertise and see if anyone has an interest in the property. You will then be required to contact by certified letter anyone who has an interest in the property. This often occurs when there is a death and there is subsequently no proper passing of title.

If you have a problem getting good title for a property, you need to contact a good title attorney who can guide you regarding what it will require to clear up the title for a property. This is a very difficult process, though. If no one owns it, it becomes hard to acquire the property. So you have to decide if the deal is potentially worth the work and expense it would take.

Also ask, "What seven or ten numbers can I dial to get the answer?" Personally, I would call my local title lawyer and say, "I have found this property and cannot find the owner. What do you recommend? In our jurisdiction, how do you get proper title?"

FORECLOSURES

A foreclosure occurs when someone lends another person money to buy property and the money is not paid back. Because the property provides the guarantee for the loan, the lender has the right to take it back, usually through a first, second, or third mortgage or tax lien.

Who lends money? In our country, mostly banks and mortgage companies provide property loans. Some governmental agencies have the authority to get a lien or judgment for nonpayment of funds owed (usually for taxes) and can foreclose on a property.

There are generally two types of foreclosures: (1) a judicial foreclosure, in which a lender has to go to court and get a judge to order the foreclosure, and (2) a deed foreclosure, or deed of trust foreclosure, in which the deed to the property is put in trust after the loan period is over. The unpaid mortgage is advertised for about 30 to 60 days. After that, the attorney or trustee forecloses on the property and takes possession of the deed through the trust.

It does not really matter to which type (judicial or deed of trust) you go. The important part is to understand the technicalities of foreclosure. For example, is the judgment final or is there a right of redemption? (That is, can the homeowner come back within six months or a year and pay off the loan and get the house back? In most states, that is not possible; when they get that property back, they have to pay the lender all the money back plus interest.)

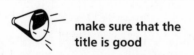

**make sure that the
title is good**

Can you be sure you will get a good title at the foreclosure sale? On whom do you rely to give you answers? I recommend you work with experts from a reputable title company. Also, get an attorney who understands foreclosures and does research well. You do not have to understand title and foreclosure law; you *do* have to know how to talk to people who can answer those questions for you.

I understand foreclosures; I am an attorney by training. However, before I buy any property, I always get a title search done or consult with my title or escrow company to make sure I am buying what I want to buy.

Legal Newspapers

Foreclosure deals are generally listed in the community's legal newspaper. In most cities and counties, foreclosures have to be advertised in the legal or regular papers a few weeks before the sale occurs. You could also call the tax assessor's office or go to the Registrar of Deeds and ask for the list of the properties going into foreclosure.

Foreclosures can be excellent deals. Some people make tons of money. Unfortunately, they come with some disadvantages. For example, often you cannot have access to the property before you buy it because the bank may have sealed it. So you have to make sure you understand the risks when you buy those foreclosures.

Tax Sales

If people do not pay their property taxes, the government taxing entity will demand payment and force a tax foreclosure. You can buy the property at a tax sale, or, in certain states, you can buy a tax certificate for the amount of the back taxes. By using a certificate, you get interest on your money or on the property. Some tax certificates pay anywhere from 10 to 30 percent interest. People buy at tax sales for two reasons:

1. They hope to get the property for the price of back taxes. For example, if a $200,000 property has $8,000 of property taxes not paid and goes to a tax sale, they want to buy it for $8,000, the amount of the back taxes. Of course, others may bid against you and raise the price. Still, you can find good deals at tax sales.

2. Many cities, counties, and states by law demand that the taxes owed and the amount bid collect a good interest rate. In certain areas, every taxing authority has rules and laws for how sales are run. Some require as much as 20 to 30 percent interest paid.

For example, the owner of a house worth $200,000 owes $8,000 in back taxes. You bid $8,000 with the intent to acquire the house for the amount of taxes only. However, your city has a one-year right of redemption rule. This means the homeowner has one year to pay back all of the taxes and interest due and redeem the property. For example, if your area's interest rate for tax liens is 20 percent, then the homeowner pays you $8,000 plus 20 percent to get the house back. If the homeowner does not pay you off within one year, you get to keep the $200,000 home. However, you cannot sell that house until the year is up.

Alternatively, you could get a property for the amount of the tax lien. You can also acquire properties by bidding on them at foreclosure auctions. The IRS also puts tax liens on property.

After you hear of a pending tax sale or foreclosure and before it happens is when you should talk to the property owners affected. Are they motivated to sell? Yes. Are they hard to talk to sometimes? Yes, because people have a psychological defense mechanism called *denial*. Sometimes people say, "No, I don't want to talk to you. I'm going to win the lottery. Someone will show up at my door and give me a million dollars. I know it's going to happen, so leave me alone."

So they are difficult to talk to, but in most cases, the things that are hardest to obtain are the sweetest. So work these foreclosures and pre-foreclosure tax sales, and develop a good source of income.

Department of Veterans Affairs

The Department of Veterans Affairs guarantees loans for veterans and publishes a list of houses it is foreclosing on. Sometimes they are good deals and occasionally they offer very favorable financing. Check with mortgage brokers for details about good deals from the Department of Veterans Affairs. (See www.shemin.com for recommendations of government real estate agencies.)

Department of Housing and Urban Development (HUD)

HUD also guarantees loans that banks make. It takes properties back for unpaid mortgages and you can bid on its foreclosed properties. Most real estate brokers and agents have access to lists of HUD foreclosures in the area. They could be a great place to find deals. (See www.shemin.com for links to HUD lists.)

Question and Answer

Q: I do not have a Realtor's license. Can I still make money in foreclosures?

A: Yes. You do not need a real estate license in most cases. I have bought and sold a lot of properties. I can put them under contract or option and sell them to somebody else. A real estate license only lets you go to the Multiple Listing Service (MLS) and make commissions off the sales of properties that are listed. This book outlines other creative ways to make money in real estate besides using MLS.

COURTS

Some real estate investors always complain about the government: the IRS, courts, regulations. But I love the government. As a real estate investor, you should love the government, too, because it is hard at work making hundreds of thousands of motivated sellers. All types of courts exist to help create motivated sellers (even when they did not think they were motivated). Here are some of them.

Codes Court

Go down to your local housing administration office to find out sched-uled dates for codes court, where landlords and investors go to defend their interests. The codes court enforces the codes and can issue fines. It can even condemn homes and have them bulldozed. Do motivated sell-ers come to these courtrooms? Yes.

The proceedings are all public record. The docket for the day is usu-ally posted outside of the courthouse. You can talk to the people while they are there and meet with lawyers, landlords, and investors who come. Every time I go to codes court, I usually find a good deal. Chances are you will, too.

Eviction Court

In every major city, evictions go to court at least a few days a week. Who shows up there? Tenants, attorneys, landlords, and managers. Owners who have a conflict on their hands and go to court to resolve it could be in the market to sell for a good price.

Know that when you go to eviction court, you may find some great deals, and you will also find better entertainment than any TV sitcom. You will also network with people you want to know. If you do not want to spend time there, you can get names, addresses, and phone numbers of people on the docket. Send them a letter that asks, "Do you have any properties you'd like to sell?" and follow up.

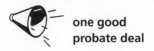
**one good
probate deal**

When the grandparents of a real estate investor I know passed away, they left behind a condominium in Florida. The family members did not want to spend time getting rid of the property and dealing with the memories, so they sold the condo to a gentleman who contacted them through a letter. He got the address from the estate probate record. The condo and other assets sold for about 60 percent of their worth. This gentleman saved the family a lot of trouble and got a great deal in the process.

Environmental Court

People who have too much junk on their properties wind up in this court. It fines people for not removing trash and not cleaning their yards. Owners of these properties can be highly motivated to sell. Go meet them, get their names, and contact them afterward. They could turn into good deals.

Divorce Court

Because divorce records are public, you can actually look up case files and see what a couple owns. Many have a home that they must sell and are often willing to take a discount just to settle the assets to get out of the marriage quickly. Get to know some divorce attorneys and show up at divorce court. You might find some good suspects there.

Estate and Probate Court

You can look in the public records where deceased persons' assets are listed. Contact the attorneys and the families and say, "Would you like to unload these properties quickly? I can help you out." Do you think you can find some deals that way?

ADVERTISING

Most real estate investors do not like to tell people what they do. They tend to be laid-back types who drive nondescript cars. If you have a quiet personality, you can get over your shyness through advertising. In my experience, businesses that have a mediocre product or service but advertise a lot bring in plenty of customers. Fast-food restaurants are a good example of that—they have poor food and mediocre service, but people spend money there every day because they see the advertisements constantly.

In real estate investing, the more you advertise, the more the word gets out, and the more deals you will get. Here are some inexpensive forms of advertising you can use.

Business Cards

Make your card stand out by printing your information on a shocking-bright paper. The wording on your card should get attention and tell people what you can do for them. "We will pay cash for your house. Can close quickly. Call me first. Call me last." You might include wording like, "If you are in trouble through foreclosure, bankruptcy, divorce, need to raise cash, need to raise money, need to sell your property quickly, call me now." Put your cell phone number on the card in a prominent place. Hand out your cards to everybody.

NETWORKING

I once attended a seminar in which I learned some information that will save you lots of time learning it yourself. It is this: When people get into financial trouble—heading for bankruptcy or foreclosure—they follow a predictable pattern of behavior. They run to their accountants, mortgage brokers, and financial planners. In desperation, they may call a Realtor and say, "Can you sell my house in three weeks?" As a last resort, they call a bankruptcy attorney.

Because of this pattern, you want to build a network of mortgage bankers, Realtors, attorneys, and accountants so that when desperate people call, they will send them to you. You can pay them cash for their house, quick-turn it, make money yourself, and possibly stop them from going bankrupt.

Investing is a lonely business. Go meet other people, talk to them, and help each other out. Here are some categories of people who can refer good deals to you.

Real Estate Agents

Real estate agents have access to the MLS and to buyers and sellers. Get to know the active agents in your targeted areas. When good deals come

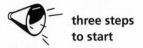

three steps to start

What will you do in the next 30 days to get some deals? Here is a three-step formula to follow:

1. Go to three auctions.
2. Make a point of meeting five investors there.
3. Take each of them to lunch and ask how they began, if they have any deals, what they are looking for, who they use for financing, and so on.

Tell them you are getting started and they will love to help you out.

their way, they will call someone, and that someone should be you. Make sure they get paid when they find deals so you keep your relationships golden. By the way, if I use agents and brokers but do not close on a property with them, I give them a check for their time until they find me something. It keeps the relationship solid.

Attorneys

Attorneys do a lot of things that can help your business: estate sales, divorces, bankruptcies. Find several active attorneys in your area and network with them.

CPAs, Accountants, Bookkeepers

When people want to do financial planning, settle their estate, sell some property, raise money, or get out of financial trouble, they turn to their trusted accountant or financial planner. These professionals often help clients dispose of their property, so get to know them and build your network.

Bankers and Mortgage Brokers

Bankers and brokers make loans to real estate people and often know where good deals are. Because they have access to funds, they can possibly finance the good deals you find. They also know lots of other investors and can help you expand your network.

BIRD-DOGGING

Bird dogs are the white dogs with brown spots that flush out rabbits and quails in a hunting situation. In real estate, bird dogs are people who can flush out deals for you.

Most successful businesses rely on many people to get things done, and everyone in the organization benefits. It is hard to be a lone wolf in the investing business; you can only look at so many deals, drive around so many neighborhoods, write so many letters, and make so many phone calls yourself.

Who can act as your bird dogs to spot good deals for you? Everyone you know, because everyone knows someone who has to sell a property at a discount or is dealing with an estate, getting a divorce, having money problems, going into bankruptcy, and so on.

Did you know that if you are a Realtor, it is illegal to pay a finder's fee? But, if you are a real estate investor, you can do what you want within the confines of the law. That means you can pay referral fees. And when you pay people, they keep coming back with more deals.

Following are several categories of people whom you can ask to be your bird dogs.

Contractors

Every contractor, big or small, is going out looking at properties that need work. They know owners and some of those owners will be motivated to sell. So contact every contractor and repair person you know and say, "If you bring me a deal that I close on, I will pay you a finder's fee."

Utility Workers

Utility workers—from the gas company, electric company, or water company—are walking and driving through neighborhoods every day. They know a lot about houses, neighborhoods, and the people with whom they deal. They may be able to say, "Hey, I know about a house that needs a lot of work. We shut the gas or the water off. And here is the owner or the address." Utility workers can be your bird dogs.

Post Office Workers

Often postal workers know more about you and your neighbors than you think they do. They know who is getting divorced, who is moving, who has to sell a house. In fact, some successful real estate investors *are* post office workers. Ask them to help you identify good deals.

Police Officers

Police officers have a tough job in the neighborhoods. They get to know about houses or property that can be sold, especially ones they just locked up because somebody did something naughty in there. They can point you to motivated sellers.

Nursing Home Workers

Our population is getting older and more people are moving into retirement, assisted living, and nursing homes. Often, people are forced to sell their property and their assets to qualify for financial assistance before going into a home.

One of my students hangs out at nursing homes to find good deals. He makes friends with the administrators, who call him and say, "Mrs. Smith has to sell her home, and the family doesn't want to deal with it. Can you help them out?" He gets a lot of good deals that way. He is not taking advantage of the situation; he is truly helping them. He discloses in writing exactly what he is doing.

THREE MORE IDEAS

I have found the following three ideas to be among the best ways to find good deals in real estate. Pick any of them, work them consistently, and you will make money.

Call Retail Finance Companies

Located in malls and shopping centers, these companies make high-risk loans to high-risk borrowers. Look them up in the Yellow Pages under finance companies. Some of their names are Associates, Beneficial, and American General. They make all kinds of loans, but also lend money to people who may not have perfect credit. Some will have local, regional, or national foreclosure centers where you can call about properties available. Often, they will sell them for the outstanding amount of the loan.

Write Letters

Whenever I send a letter to a prospect, I always follow up with a phone call. That alone triples my response rate. Write first, then call and ask questions like, "How long have you had the property? Would you be interested in selling? Can I help out?"

Join Real Estate Associations

Most major cities have a real estate association and/or a landlord association. Who attends the meetings? Investors, landlords, and people who find good deals. Associations are great sources of education, too. At www.shemin.com, we provide a list of real estate associations. Network at their meetings and you will find everything you need to become a successful real estate investor.

WHAT IS ONE DEAL WORTH?

What if you find that great deal—a house you can turn over, flip, or wholesale? You make $8,000 or $12,000 or $20,000 in a short time by selling it soon after you buy it. What is one deal worth to you? (See Chapter 7.)

What if you find one great deal, say a house you can buy and hold? You borrow $100,000, rent out the house, and pay for it in 15 years. By then it's worth $300,000 and you have made thousands. (See Chapter 6.)

What if you lease-option a house? With this method you get three paydays. The tenants pay you up front with option money. You lease it out every month and have $300 to $500 extra cash coming in every month. And when they buy the house, you make another $15,000. (See Chapter 8.)

Returns like these are possible with great, and even good, deals. If you make it part of your business plan to commit to search out such deals, I promise you that you will become a successful real estate investor.

Next you'll learn about the numerous ways you can create multiple real estate profit centers.

chapter 6

multiple real estate profit centers

Big shots are only little shots who keep shooting.
—Christopher Morley

During my first several years of real estate investing, I knew of only one way to make money in real estate—buying and holding. That is, buying and renting property and collecting rents. Then I learned about wholesaling (or flipping), lease optioning, referring contractors and legal services, and more. I started getting little checks, then medium-sized checks, and finally big checks.

I will help you do the same. But you have to decide how many checks you want and from how many sources. You have to open your mind to not only one, two, or three avenues of income, but to many streams of real estate income. To help you do that, in this chapter, I'll lead you to the various "streams" where the "fishing" is good. You can pick and choose among them—start with one way, then, as your career progresses, you will want to add others.

WHOLESALING, OR FLIPPING, STRATEGY

Did you realize almost everything you buy is wholesaled, or flipped, including your chairs, your furniture, your televisions, and more? In

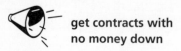

get contracts with no money down

When I started in real estate in the early 1990s, a gentleman named Larry, about the same age as I (27 or 28 at the time), visited owners of office buildings around downtown Nashville, Tennessee, and asked, "What would you sell your building for?" If they said, "Two million dollars," he'd reply, "What's the least you'd take for the office building? Can you do any better?" They'd say $1.8 million and he'd get an option to buy that building for $1.8 million for six months without putting any money down.

Then Larry would run an ad in a German newspaper inviting Germans to invest in American real estate in Nashville. This ad generated calls from several overseas investors. To follow up, he would send them a photo of the building with all the details spelled out, including rents and answers to questions that an investor would ask about the property. He also included some comparable sales on the flyer. Then he would ask, "What would you pay for a building like this?" They might respond with $2.4 million or $2.2 million, or whatever. Larry would then get a contract and work with a good commercial closing attorney. After he closed the deal, he would make anywhere from $200,000 to $800,000 on each building. In just a few years, he flipped or wholesaled about seven of them and made a lot of money. However, he had a lawsuit served against him because a German investor said, "We thought you were representing us. We did not know you were wholesaling and making money."

What is the lesson here? You must write into all of your contracts a statement such as "I do not represent you or your interests." If Larry had included that statement in his contracts, he wouldn't have been sued, or he would have won the lawsuit.

these cases, a businessperson went to companies in China, Japan, Korea, or even locally and put them under contract to make items, then sold those items to a retail store for a marked-up price.

Similarly, car dealerships put their cars on a lot for sale. They get vehicles from the manufacturer without putting any money down. They have finance plans with the manufacturers for, say, $20,000 per car, then they sell that car to a buyer for $25,000. That's called *wholesaling, quick turning,* or *flipping.* Most industries are doing business this way, including real estate.

This is such an important strategy. I devote an entire chapter to it, Chapter 7.

LEASE-OPTIONING STRATEGY

One of the best ways to control or rent property is through lease option-ing. Consider leasing commercial property, houses, vacation property, duplexes, land. Instead of borrowing money to buy a property, thereby getting your name (and all the liability that comes with it) on the deed, consider leasing it for 1 year, 5 years, possibly 50 years.

Think of it this way: If 10 years ago you had locked into 10-year leases on every house in your neighborhood, what leases for $1,000 a month now probably leased for $200 a month a decade ago. Therefore, if you originally leased property for $200 and rented it today for $1,000, you would be making $800 a month.

When you lease with the option to buy, you are locking in the lease for a set number of years as well as having the choice to buy it. Remem-ber, you are not obligated to buy the property, but you do have the right to. When you lease-option property, you control it. You can re-lease it, buy it, option to buy it, or sell it for more than what your option price was. The sky is the limit.

Like wholesaling, this, too, is an important strategy that warrants its own chapter. Read more about it in Chapter 8.

BUY-FIX-AND-SELL STRATEGY

Think like a real estate wholesaler getting properties ready for retail sale. Find houses that need painting, cleaning, and fixing, then sell them at retail price. On a single-family home, for example, you should make an average of $12,000 to $25,000 for a house that would sell in the $50,000 to $100,000 range. If you have a house in the $100,000 to $150,000 range, you should make $20,000 to $30,000 after you buy it, fix it up, and sell it. If it is in the $200,000 to $300,000 range, you should make between $20,000 and $50,000. For commercial buildings that sell between $0.5 million and $2 million, you could make from $30,000 up to as much as $80,000, depending on your capital, your time, and the overhead involved. However, if you can't make a good amount of money on the deal, it may not be worth your time. Make sure you get paid not only for the use of your time, but also for the use of your capital.

Know the Costs

When you buy a house to fix up and sell, you need to know the following costs:

- Carrying costs
- Taxes
- Insurance
- Repairs (give yourself room for cost overruns)
- Transaction costs (closing costs to buy it, closing costs to sell it, commissions)

Calculate at what price you think you can sell the house, how long it will take you to sell it, your cost of capital, and your payment to yourself. If you are spending 20 hours a month working at the house or running back and forth, what's your time worth? $10? $20? $100 an hour? Multiply that number into the equation to decide whether this buy-fix-and-sell property will be profitable for you.

I have met a lot of real estate investors who have told me stories like this one: "I bought a house for $50,000, spent $20,000 fixing it, and sold it for $90,000. I made $20,000. It only took me a year and a half. I worked on it every day, six days a week, did all the painting and carpeting myself." I say "Congratulations. You just bought yourself a $6-an-hour job."

That is not what savvy real estate investors do. Your job is to find good deals, put them together, and sell them. If you want to be a drywaller or a painter, then spend time learning how to do these skills, especially in the beginning. There's nothing wrong with that. In fact, many investors start by doing their own work because they have to hold on to their money. However, remember your goal: Do you want to be a cleaner, painter, and drywaller, or do you want to be an investor who makes money?

To summarize, make sure that there's a big enough margin in the deal for your profit, your overhead, your time, and your cost of capital. Also, verify that your contractors' bids are accurate and that you can rely on reputable repair people. Allow extra time and money for this strategy because repairs always take longer than you think.

Dealing with Contractors

When people buy property to fix up, their biggest complaint is dealing with contractors. That's why I suggest you make sure that every repair bid is in writing, that you have a fixed finish date for each part of the job, and that you never give your contractors more money than the work that has been done. Draw out payment every week as they do the work; never advance them too much. If you do, they won't finish the job because they've already been paid.

In addition, if they don't finish by the date they promised in writing, have a per-day penalty, just as the government has. When city, county, and state governments build new facilities, they use hold-backs and per-day penalties because, for every day your property is unfinished, it is a day you cannot sell or rent it. You're losing money, so you need to deduct a per-day penalty from the money you owe the contractor. Again, have everything in writing, and most important, make sure that you are working with referred, licensed, bonded, and insured contractors.

Use Other People's Money

The best way to buy and hold (or even buy and fix up) property is through other people's money (OPM). Remember, I introduced you to this strategy in Chapter 3. I want to expand on that idea a little here.

You could own 10 houses in your name and be on the hook for 10 loans at $100,000 apiece. Alternatively, you could get a partner who puts up the $1 million. Instead of putting your name on the loan or mortgage and using your credit, use OPM. Have a silent partner with whom you can work. You make all of the decisions, use your energy to fix up and sell the property, pay back your partner's initial investment, and split the profits. Your silent partner holds the property in his or her name, and you receive a written agreement that's filed at the courthouse. For example, the agreement might state you each have a 50 percent interest in the income and equity of the property. When that property sells, you are entitled to half of the profit. When it's rented, you get half of the rent and pay half of the expenses. How much money comes out of your pocket? None.

Be sure to carefully analyze any deal you make, running through all the numbers regarding what comes in and what goes out. That way, both you and your partner have a clear idea on how the money will flow. Warn your partner (as I am warning you) that it is likely that you will spend more money than you think and always make less money than you predict, as in any business—and especially in real estate. However, you will make money if you do it right. Occasionally, a deal will make a lot more money than you thought. It all works out.

Offer an Incentive

To make the partnership attractive, you can give the person who puts up the money the advantages of writing off expenses and depreciation on his or her taxes. You may want to form a legal corporation or partnership so you can give your partner certain income tax benefits, yet you still own half of the property and half of the income.

You might be able to negotiate with your partner for more than 50 percent of the profit and income. Just do what is fair and right. Remember the saying "Pigs get fat, hogs get slaughtered." I believe there is plenty of money for everyone involved, if you are able to find good deals.

BUYING-AND-HOLDING STRATEGY

When you decide to buy and hold property, you have the advantage of building a lot of wealth because every month the debt goes down, the property appreciates, and the cash comes in. Would you like to have several rental properties that generate thousands of dollars a month so you can use that money to pay expenses, pay off debts, and have extra cash flow every month? If you don't want to manage the property, you can hire a management company and manage the manager. You can be free from dealing with tenants and still receive income every month.

Owning property remains one of the best wealth builders available. It can be a great way to build up an education or a retirement fund for children, grandchildren, or favorite relatives. You can even buy a house in their names and, in about 15 years, they will have a paid asset worth a lot more than you paid for it.

Understand, though, that buying and holding property can be a roller-coaster ride. Sometimes properties are vacant; sometimes tenants and repairs create headaches for you. However, over the long term, if they generate enough cash flow and enough equity, they will make you rich.

FINANCING MORTGAGES AS A STRATEGY

Every time you buy or sell a property, it is likely that there is some type of mortgage on it. You can profit from these mortgages. For many years, while I was buying or selling properties, I referred between 30 and 80 people a year to a particular mortgage company. After a while, I decided to become a mortgage originator (i.e., someone who finds people needing mortgages). This mostly requires filling out some paperwork. The processor actually processes the mortgages, but the originator gets a fee ranging anywhere from 30 to 70 percent of the mortgage amounts for finding customers. On a $100,000 loan, for example, that fee could be 1 point ($1,000), 2 points ($2,000), or even from 3 to 5 points (from $5,000 to $7,000).

Start by becoming affiliated with a mortgage company that does good work and that hires people who are honest and dependable. By becoming a mortgage originator, every time a mortgage is completed, you earn those fees.

Owner Financing

If you live in the world of real estate, you will find people who either give you or already have owner-financing notes. As an example, you could put $1,000 down on a $100,000 price, and the lender would give you $99,000 on a $100,000 purchase for 30 years at 10 percent interest. You can then broker that loan and earn a fee for doing it. Start by calling on people who buy those mortgages (they advertise in local newspapers, or ask around for referrals), and ask, "What would you pay for this type of loan?" They might reply, "We're going to discount it. We'll pay $94,000." Then you call the property owners and ask, "What's the least amount you would take if we could get that cash in your hands right now?" They reply, "We'll take $90,000." You write up the contracts, then have the mortgage company that is buying the loan arrange the legalities and close it for you. They pay you $94,000, and you pay the property owners $90,000. You will make about $4,000 on that mortgage transaction.

robert's tip

Remember, any time you make money at something, be sure to disclose your role to your clients by saying, "I recommend this mortgage company. I'm an originator. I get paid for recommending the loan to you."

Mortgages as a Source of Income

Mortgages are bought and sold every minute in the United States. In fact, when you first got a loan on your home, the bank or loan company probably sold it immediately. Stop letting them make all the money and get into the action, too.

In addition to being a mortgage originator, I also buy loans. If you have a pending mortgage opportunity, go to www.shemin.com, or call and tell us what you've got. We'll either make a bid on it or find others to buy your loans.

Some people make a living brokering notes like this by running ads and finding owner-held financing. When you're talking to potential investors and sellers, simply ask "By the way, do you have owner-held financing or do you know anyone who has it and would like to sell it?" When they answer yes, ask for details. Write down the basic terms of the note [e.g., type of mortgage (first or second mortgage), characteristics of the property behind it, value of the property, terms (amount, payment, principal, interest, years left on the note, who has signed it), and credit-worthiness of the noteholder]. Then ask us for a quote on the note. We'll help you determine what your profit can be.

OTHER AVENUES

Being a Real Estate Agent

What source of income first comes to mind when *real estate* is mentioned? Making money as a real estate agent or broker involves putting buyers and sellers together and carrying offers between them. The average real estate commission in the United States is generally between 5 and 8 percent of the sale. For example, if a sales price is $100,000 with a 6 percent commission, the agent or broker earns $6,000. Often, however, there are two agent/brokers, one representing the buyer and the other representing the seller, so the commission gets split, dispersing $3,000 to each.

The disadvantages of being a real estate agent/broker include requirements such as being licensed, meeting educational standards, paying fees, and carrying liability insurance coverage.

Of course, being an agent/broker has an advantage. You have access to the Multiple Listing Service (MLS), which lists all houses for sale in the retail real estate market. You might have access to a real estate office and its up-to-date technology, and also have contact with other agents and resources who can lead you to sales.

Consulting

After you have been investing in real estate for a few years, you become an expert and can actually earn money from others (e.g., bankers, other investors, newcomers) for your consulting. People will ask you questions all the time anyway, so consider developing an avenue of income that helps you profit from sharing your advice.

Partnering

Partnering (people with different skills and assets working together to form successful real estate ventures) is another path for making money in real estate. You can partner in almost limitless ways: with money, capital, credit, expertise, repairs, and management. Decide what your skills are and stick to them, but also find partners to fill in areas where you lack expertise.

One of the biggest mistakes people make in any business, especially real estate investing, is trying to do everything themselves. Are you prepared to be a finance expert, a real estate acquisition expert, a contractor, a property manager, an accountant, a bookkeeper, and an eviction

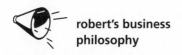

robert's business philosophy

Ask yourself why you want to get into real estate investing. Sure, you want to make a lot of money, but real estate investing is more about freedom.

I urge you to follow my business philosophy, which is to do nothing. That is right—nothing. If I have other professionals doing their jobs properly, I can do next to nothing and profit from it.

For instance, you may have money or credit but little time. Why not locate partners to find deals for you; use *their* time and energy and *your* money or credit. What if you do not have money or credit but have lots of time to look for deals? Partner with people who have money or credit. In the same manner, you can partner with a contractor for your rehabilitation projects or with a management company that manages the rental properties it finds for you.

agent? Are you an attorney or an appraiser? You are wise to get to know those who can help.

Managing Real Estate

You can make money in real estate as a manager mainly by managing tenants. In residential or commercial management, managers generally earn a percentage of rents collected and sometimes a percentage of repairs. Alternatively, they can get commissions (anywhere from 3 to 15 percent) for locating tenants, signing leases, negotiating new leases, and signing and leasing property.

I must warn you, managing properties requires a tremendous amount of detailed work and can be stressful. Unless you do a lot of it, it's not even very profitable. If you enjoy managing people, then do it, by all means. If not, you can always hire a manager, then manage the manager. Use this approach as another source of real estate income.

Tax Liens

Tax liens usually have to be paid off first when a piece of real estate is sold or foreclosed on. The government has the first claim on the property, even above banks or lenders who have financed a mortgage. Tax liens pay good rates of return, so you might want to familiarize yourself with this concept.

Judgments and Liens

Investors who are active in real estate or landlords who have a lot of tenants will experience times when people owe them money and they have to collect judgments and liens.

To save on expenses, you could learn how to collect your own judgments and liens. To create another avenue of income, you could take it a step further. Here's how it works. If someone owes $50,000 on his or her property, a judge has put a lien on it, and it hasn't been collected on for five years, you could possibly negotiate the option or the contract to buy that property for $5,000, which is the amount of the judgment. You would approach the owner and say, "Look, you owe $50,000 on this house, but if you pay us $15,000 next week, we'll wipe out the remaining debt. We'll forgive it, forget it, extinguish it." If you did that, you could earn more than $10,000.

Foreclosures

One of the most popular sources of income in real estate is foreclosures. When a house is foreclosed on, it means that a homeowner has borrowed money that he or she cannot repay. The lender takes possession of the property, but in most cases the lender is really interested in recouping the loan's principal balance and expenses incurred.

If a property is worth $100,000 and the principal balance plus expenses due the lender is $100,000, stay away from that deal! However, if that property is worth $162,000 and the lender only wants $100,000 to cover costs, I suggest that you get control of that foreclosure and find out how to profit from it.

You can go to a number of places to find out about foreclosure deals: banks, mortgage companies, government agencies, private lenders, and tax agencies. Remember, though, real estate investors are not out to take advantage of anyone. If you cannot help the person being foreclosed, you do not want to get involved. You are not in the business to get people to sign over houses they do not want to sign over. That would be a bad deal—you never want to get involved in one.

Title and Escrow Closing Fees

Some savvy real estate investors and Realtors have started generating income from title and escrow closing fees. When they get involved in numerous closings, they can make legal and ethical agreements to get marketing or consulting fees for their efforts. Investors might even be able to use another company's computers or office space in exchange for bringing customers on board. This often-overlooked source of income can add significantly to your fountain of wealth.

Buying and Selling Discounted Notes

When you buy (or broker at a discount) a note, you give those people holding notes on properties the opportunity to get their money without waiting the full term of the loan. You might know someone who made arrangements to sell his or her house for $100,000 and took back an $80,000 mortgage. At 30 years at 10 percent interest, he or she may be making $700 a month on that note, with 25 years left to pay. Here is what you say: "Instead of waiting another 25 years to get the rest of your $80,000, how would you like $60,000 in cash in the next few weeks?" Someone needing funds might go for that offer immediately.

A number of people make money by buying notes, so why not make some sales commissions by bringing together buyers and sellers of those notes?

Maintenance and Repair

Owning real estate inevitably involves repairing and maintaining property. If you regularly contract for lawn care, roofing, new appliances, and carpet cleaning and installers, you know which companies provide good prices and service. You are probably willing to recommend those companies to your associates, but it makes sense to make money by setting up a system of referral fees first.

Generally, before I refer a good contractor or maintenance person, I make a contractual agreement that guarantees me from 10 to 20 percent of the bid for a job. Because I am providing work that person would not have had without me, I should earn a commission for that service.

Legal Services

If you are in any business in the United States, especially real estate, you are going to need attorneys. Using prepaid legal services, you can profit from other people needing attorneys by participating in a national legal referral system. By selling prepaid legal expense plans, you can develop another source of income. (More on this in Chapter 13.)

Appraisals

Generally, any time a property purchase is being financed by a loan, it needs to be appraised. You could become a professional appraiser—provided you are careful about conflict of interest. Also, you might refer appraisers and, when it is legal and ethical, earn commissions from those referrals.

Insurance

Never buy property without proper insurance, which may include title insurance, liability insurance, fire insurance, and insurance plans specific to commercial property. Someone has to broker and make commissions from all that insurance. Perhaps you could get an insurance license or develop a marketing and referral system with certain trusted agents. That will lead to still another avenue of real estate–related income.

Ancillary Services and Profit Centers

Ancillary services are part of buying, fixing up, and renting property. They can include furniture rental, cable TV rental, Internet service, tenant services, even restaurants. You could generate different forms of income from all of these services by charging referral fees for anything your tenants or clients could possibly need.

For example, if your tenants and clients need a satellite or computer hookup, a moving service, a rental truck, or whatever, you would likely refer them to service providers you know; you might as well get paid for it. You will learn more about these various sources of real estate income in the chapters that follow.

SEVEN SECRETS FOR GETTING PAID

1. *Residual income.*   The beauty of buying and holding property is that it generates residual income. One of the problems with wholesaling, or buying, fixing, and selling property, is the absence of ongoing or residual income. Therefore, if you turn a property and make a few thousand dollars, you still have no money coming in the next month from that property. Remember, residual income creates happiness (RICH). One of your themes for real estate investing should be RICH.

   How would you like to have the best of both worlds? Let me explain. A few years ago, a student located 20 duplexes in disrepair. The owners were motivated to sell because the buildings were run-down. They were willing to sell them for $20,000 each, owner's terms.

   Each unit was actually worth about $40,000 or $50,000, so my student put the property under contract for $20,000 and flipped most of the units to me for about $28,000 each. My student made $160,000 ($8,000 × 20) by quick-turning that deal. I received a good deal because I got property worth more than the price I paid. The original sellers got what they wanted, too. In fact, one of the sellers wrote us a letter thanking us for taking those horrible duplexes off his hands. We then wholesaled these units to another investor and made about $60,000 ($3,000 per duplex × 20). The end buyer of the duplexes fixed them up and raised the rents tremendously. In a matter of three years, the duplexes increased in value to $120,000 each. The end buyer later sold those 20 properties and made more than $1 million, all because of the deal my student found. Some might think I should be upset by that result because I only made $60,000 and the end buyer made $1 million. That did not seem fair. I learned from that experience to develop a strategy of sitting down with prospective property buyers and walking them through the numbers, saying, "Mr. and Mrs. Investor, you're going to buy these duplexes for $60,000, and they'll be worth $100,000 or more in a few years. You'll make a lot of money. Isn't that great? One way I get paid for bringing these great opportunities to you is through a fee. It doesn't come out of your pocket until you sell or refinance the property. My fee would be five percent of the sales price whenever you sell or refinance these properties. That could be in a year or two, or even three years from now.

"We'll put a note against the property and record it at the courthouse. The lawyer will handle all of this. Whenever you refinance or sell the property, I get an extra fee for helping you get this great deal in the first place. Realize that you'll make most or all of the money—about $20,000 per building—and I'll only get, say, $4,000, assuming it sells for $90,000 or so." This approach is almost like getting a second mortgage recorded against the property with your name, address, and phone number. Because of the recording, the buyers cannot sell that property or refinance it until they pay the fee.

Ask for this kind of deal every time you wholesale or sell a property. Have your attorney draw up the paperwork. You will not always get the purchaser's agreement, but what if you get it a few times? You then get paid again on the property you have already received payment on.

Be sure to disclose everything in writing and check with your own attorney to make sure you can do it. I have done this a few times and enjoyed getting a call or letter stating, "Please sign this paper. We need to pay you your $9,000 because we can't sell the property or refinance it until you release your lien."

What if the sale took place 10 years previously and the property increased in value to $1 million? Five percent of that would be $50,000—not bad. Suppose you request this residual income and the prospective buyer asks, "Why should I let you get paid again when the property sells?" Your reply would be, "How much do you think this will be worth five years from now? If it's worth $100,000 then and you're buying it for $60,000 now, you're going to make $40,000. So do you really mind paying someone $5,000 to make $40,000? If that isn't a good deal for you, I know a lot of other buyers who'd like to get into this deal."

The buyer might say, "No way. I'm greedy; I'm not going to give you anything. I want to make all of the money." Then you make a choice: Either wholesale the property to that person without taking the residual income, or move on to somebody else. However, I promise you this: If you never *ask* for the residual, you will never get it. If you ask for it every time, you will get it sometimes. That "sometimes" could be worth $2,000, $5,000, $10,000, or even $20,000.

2. *Make three offers.*   Whenever you make an offer on a property, don't make just one offer. Make three. For example, if the sellers want $100,000 for their house, make one offer for $64,500 in cash. Make a second offer with $1,000 down at $65,922. Make a third offer with nothing down and $800 a month for $68,422. You have given them three choices: the cash offer being the lowest, the second one with terms a little higher, and the third one with terms higher still. When you sell a property, do the same thing: Say, "If you give me cash, pay me a wholesale flip fee, and agree to a residual fee, it's this particular price; if you don't give me that, it's another price."

3. *Become a mortgage broker.*   Some states require a license, certificates, and educational classes to become a mortgage broker whereas others don't. The same is true to be a mortgage originator. Consult with your attorney or mortgage company, or call the mortgage department at the departments of commerce and insurance in your state and find out the requirements.

Generally, you can affiliate with several mortgage brokers and become an originator without too many regulations. Mainly, you want to affiliate with reputable brokerage companies and get referral fees from them. That's how to develop another source of real estate revenue. You can get referral fees from contractors and title companies, too. Just make sure they are run by honest people who deliver great service.

4. *Put service before money.*   More important than making lots of money is delivering quality service to your clients. If you give good service, you *will* make money; if you give bad service, you will be out of business. Remember, always disclose any referral or relationship fee in writing to your clients.

5. *Choose a geographic focus.*   As a beginner, should you concentrate on one small area, view the whole city as your territory, or consider the whole state or country as your domain? The answer: Do what you feel comfortable with.

Initially, I picked a moderate-income neighborhood in Nashville on which to focus. It took me only a few weeks to know the neighborhood and the prices in it. However, I realized the people who make the most money have more guts than beginners, and they make bigger deals. Before long, I expanded beyond the first targeted neighborhood. I now view the whole world as my territory, so when I travel and go on vacation, I often find a deal, then wholesale it or lease-option it.

I suggest that you first concentrate on smaller deals in a certain area before branching out into, for instance, large apartment buildings in exotic locations. However, be careful not to spend all your time chasing elephants—big deals that never happen.

6. *Find the right advisors.*   How do you find title and mortgage brokering companies that will do double flips, wholesaling, and creative simultaneous closings? I share the names of attorneys around the country who probably will close deals and/or know others who do. I also suggest contacting real estate associations for referrals.

I warn you, though, that you will find some Realtors who know nothing about wholesaling and lease optioning, renting to own, flipping, zero percent financing, brokering mortgages, and so on. These people belong to a group that says you can't do these things, because they have never done them themselves. Do not listen to them! It reminds me of my friend who has been divorced six times yet loves to give out relationship advice.

everyone makes money

In the world of investing, you want everybody to make money. Actually, I like my clients to make a little more money than I do because the way to really profit in any business is to have repeat clients.

Maybe I only make $8,000 to wholesale a property when I could have made $12,000. However, if my clients bought it from me, fixed it up, sold it, and made $30,000, they will come back. My lawyer friends have a saying: If you're going to rip someone off, do it once, do it big, and leave the country. Some real estate investors like to rip people off in little ways, and that is stupid! They don't make much money, and they have unhappy clients.

Another group of advice givers includes people who have failed miserably at something and love to tell you how bad the whole idea was. You may go to a real estate investor or a Realtor who bought a house one time, did not follow good policies and procedures, and lost money. They quickly tell you flipping will not work.

A third group that gives advice is made up of experts who have successfully worked in a certain field for years and years. They know exactly what they are talking about; they have encountered a full range of positive and negative situations. Listen to *them*. Make sure your advice comes from people in *this* category.

7. *Invest in your own home.*   Your best real estate investment is your own home because you now know you can buy a home for less than what it is worth. Let me give you an example. You could buy a home worth $100,000 for $70,000. Instead of having a $100,000 mortgage, it will be $70,000 (or $68,000 with a $2,000 down payment). Your payment will be about $550 a month, depending on the interest rate. After living there for two years, you can

robert's tip

One of the best deals going is finding a good deal on your own home, living in it for about two years (check with your accountant for residency requirements), then selling it and making money tax-free.

sell it for up to $250,000, make a profit, and not pay any taxes on it (in the United States). If you're married, you can sell it for up to $0.5 million after two years or more.

Suppose that after two years, your home appreciates quickly and becomes worth $200,000. You find another deal, keeping the same level of mortgage payment but making money each time. That's tax-free income.

WALKING DOWN THE WIDEST AVENUE

I know I've given you a lot to think about in this chapter. My intent was not to overwhelm you with information, but to encourage you to become enthusiastic about the number of options available to you for making money in real estate. In the next chapter, I focus on a single strategy— wholesaling—because I consider it to be one of the most lucrative.

chapter 7

the whole story on wholesaling

You can never go broke making a profit.
—Anonymous

One of the best ways for people to begin in real estate and to make money without using their own money is wholesaling properties, or "flipping" them.

Why wholesale? You could get into rehabbing, rentals, buying and holding property, but all of these have drawbacks. If you're rehabbing properties, you never have enough money to buy the property, hold it, fix it, and wait to sell it. If you have rental property, you have to buy it, fix it, manage it, put up with the tenants, and you won't have cash until you sell it or refinance it. Buying and holding requires borrowing money. The only time you make any serious money in real estate is when you sell or refinance. Why not skip the borrowing, fixing, and managing by wholesaling it? Get in and get out; flip them and make cash. Do that for six months or a year until you have a bunch of cash in your bank account. Then you can think about buying, holding, fixing, and renting.

Basically, *wholesaling* means getting paid for finding a good deal. Not owning it, not buying it, not taking title to it, not borrowing money, not dealing with contractors, not having really any liability if you structure your contracts right. You strictly get paid for finding good deals. How can you sell something or get paid for something you don't own? Well, just about everything in the world is flipped, or wholesaled.

For example, you go to a car dealership to buy a brand-new car. The salesperson conveniently offers you financing for that car, even though the dealership doesn't own it. It has a contract or an option with the car's manufacturer. If the dealership sells it to you for $40,000 and had a floor-plan agreement to pay the manufacturer $34,000, the dealership makes $6,000 (plus a potential bonus for selling several cars). The car dealership just "flipped" you a car.

The chair you're sitting on, the desk you work at, the couch you sit on at home, the television set you watch—just about everything you buy is wholesaled, or flipped. A friend of mine locates vacant lots for large retailers. He might, for example, visit a farmer who owns property on the edge of town and ask to put the land under contract for $100,000 with a contingency. His contingency clause usually says that the contract or option to buy is contingent on his partners' approval, his partners being the company to whom he is going to "wholesale" the property. Then he meets with the retail people and asks, "What would you pay for this land to put one of your big stores on?" They may be willing to pay $200,000, so he takes the company's $200,000 and gives the farmer (or the commercial broker who represents the farmer) $100,000. They close the deal and my friend, in effect, gets paid for finding the deal.

---

brainstorming worksheet

What type of deals do you want to wholesale?

_____
_____
_____

What other types of goods, assets, or services could you wholesale?

_____
_____
_____

The farmer in this case was happy to receive $100,000. The company wanted the land to build a superstore, factory, or office and was happy to pay $200,000. My friend made $100,000 for finding the deal. He used a contract to buy it for $100,000. He had another contract to sell it to the company for $200,000. The attorney or title company took both contracts, closed the deal, and paid my friend $100,000 for putting a willing buyer and able seller together. He didn't spend or use his own money or credit.

COMPONENTS OF WHOLESALING

You can do a lot to increase your chances of success when wholesaling real estate. Become familiar with the following components.

Get Preapprovals for Funding

Never sign a contract with buyers until they're preapproved. Get a written verification that this transaction has been preapproved by a mortgage company or bank, or have the buyers show written proof that they have adequate funds available. By doing that, you can make sure the probability of deals falling through drops drastically.

According to a survey of more than 1,000 investors I conducted recently, over 40 percent of all contracts for sale fall through because the buyer could not get the cash or financing to close. You can avoid this by requiring confirmation, in writing, that your buyer has been preapproved or has the cash in hand.

 **think about it**

How many times have people told you they were going to do something, but didn't do it? It's frustrating, isn't it? That's why I suggest making it your business policy and procedure to put every agreement *in writing*. When lenders say they will lend you money, get their statements *in writing*. When other investors say they have the cash to do your deal, get proof *in writing*. When contractors say they'll fix something at a property by a certain date, get it *in writing*. When people say they'll pay you some money, get that promise *in writing*. Can you think back to an incident where this would have served you well? Make it a habit now.

Insist on an Inspection Clause

Insist on putting tight inspection clauses into your contracts. Here's an example of this: Say I want to buy a house from Mr. Motivated Seller who's moving out of the country. The house is worth $200,000 and he'll sell it to me for $100,000. It's the deal of the century, right? The contract I present requires an inspection and approval before closing. That means I can back out of the contract anytime before closing, subject to inspecting the property. The seller might protest and won't accept that condition. I reply, "It's a vacant home. What if kids break the windows? What if there's a fire or flood? What if something happens? Do you mean I've got to buy it even if the windows are broken and the walls are torn out? I insist on including that clause if I'm going to close on this property." If the seller still doesn't agree, I'm faced with a business decision: If it's a good enough deal, I might take the risk and close on it, despite the seller not agreeing to guarantee the house's condition. If I know I can sell it and make a profit, I go ahead.

Include a Clear Title Clause

Here's a good example to illustrate why it's important to get a clear title clause in the contract. You want to buy a house for $20,000. You have it under contract; it's a good deal. You're planning to rehab it and then sell it. Fixing it up will cost $5,000, so you'll have $25,000 in it and can sell it for $50,000 or $60,000. Your net would be $30,000—and that's a killer deal, right? But when you go to close on this deal, you find out the seller doesn't have clear title to the property and therefore can't pass it on. (Note: Always make sure that the seller has and can pass on a valid title. And always get a title insurance policy when you buy a property.)

What do you do? Start by talking to a decision maker at the bank, even call the president or head attorney and ask why this isn't closing. Clear up the title issue before signing any paperwork. You might consider including in your contract a clause that asks for liquidated damages (i.e., you receive compensation if this transaction can't close). Note that the inclusion of liquidated damages clauses is not valid in a lot of states, so talk with your attorney and ask how to avoid losing a deal due to an unclear title. It will depend on the answers to these questions: Was the contract contingent on being able to pass good title? Has the bank signed the contract?

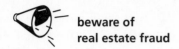

beware of real estate fraud

Say you have a contract for $100,000. The investor who wants to buy this contract is willing to pay you $140,000, then fix up the property and sell it for $210,000. You're going to wholesale it and make $40,000, right?

You get ready to close on this deal within seven days. All of a sudden, you find out the seller can't pass on the title. But the buyer you've lined up has a contract with *you,* not the seller. The buyer is furious when she finds out. She calls and says, "I'm buying the house from you. Now you tell me it's not yours, that you're buying from this other guy. You didn't say that. You told me you were selling the house. I have a contract with *you.*" You just attempted to sell something you didn't own; you may have committed fraud.

What should you do to prevent this from happening? Include a clear title clause in your contract. It would say, "This contract is contingent on being able to pass good title." I put this statement in big bold print, in plain English, at the top of every contract to protect myself against fraud.

If the deal falls through, you may decide to take steps to sue the bank, with or without having a liquidated damages clause. For example, I would have made $30,000 on this transaction, so the damages would be at least $30,000, plus attorney fees.

Put All Disclosures in Writing

Disclosure means to make it clear to everyone involved in a transaction what you are doing. Certainly the one clear defense for fraud is disclosure. You have to be up front, careful, ethical, and honest in all your business transactions.

About the same year I started investing in real estate in Nashville, another guy a year older than I also started in real estate. I bought little houses and duplexes and I didn't understand wholesaling. I went out and borrowed money; I didn't use any of my own. I bought property and rented it out for more than the mortgage and did well. Great business, right? Tenants, cash flow, equity—awesome. I bought little houses and properties, as you might do in the beginning.

But this other guy had more guts than I did. He went around to some of the biggest commercial buildings in Nashville, and asked owners what they'd sell their buildings for. Most said they weren't for sale. But he persisted and asked, "Well if someone were to buy your building, what would you sell it for?" One small-building owner said, "We'd like $4 million for our building." The real estate investor replied, "Great. Will you sign a contract giving me a right to buy it for $4 million while I get all my partners and financing together?" This is typical in commercial property. His contract had a contingency clause so that if he couldn't buy it, he could withdraw from the contract.

Then he spent about $200 to run an ad in Germany stating commercial real estate buildings in Tennessee were available as a good investment. Some German investors who wanted to be property owners in the United States responded to the ad. They flew over to Nashville, he took them around to all the buildings on which he had contracts and asked, "What would you pay for this building?" They said they'd pay about $4.9 million, for example, on that particular building. He had a contract drawn up and signed. He put the deal together, went to closing, and repeated these steps. In two or three years, he made over $4 million by flipping or wholesaling about six buildings to German investors. He never owned the buildings, but he earned money by bringing the buyers and sellers together.

However, he got into trouble. He did something you're not going to do. The German investors thought that he was representing them, and they didn't realize he was making all this money, so they sued him and actually won a settlement, though not a full settlement for everything they'd requested. His mistake was in not disclosing everything he was doing in his contracts. He needed to explain in writing that he was putting the property under contract to resell it for a profit, so the sellers would know he's the middleman, not the buyer. His contract with the German buyers should have read: "I am a real estate investor. I don't represent you or your interests. I buy and sell property for a profit, and this contract is contingent on my being able to pass good title. I may or may not have good title right now." If that investor had done this with the German investors, he would have won in court because he would have disclosed exactly what he was doing. The German investors would have no doubt bought the buildings despite such a clause; they knew they would make a lot of money. The real estate investor who flipped, or wholesaled, the property still kept millions of dollars of property.

 **think about it**

What type of properties would you like to wholesale?

- Land
- Vacation property
- Apartment buildings
- Condos
- Homes
- Commercial property

If you spent 5 to 15 hours a week building a network of motivated sellers and potential buyers, how many properties could you wholesale in . . .

90 days? _____

Six months? _____

One year? _____

If you never make an offer on a piece of property, you will never own one. With proper disclosures and a contingency clause, your risk is minimized in making offers on good deals.

How many offers could you make this week? _____

This month? _____

Each month? _____

This year? _____

Have Lots of Deals Pending

At any given time, how many deals do most successful investors have in play? I probably have 14 to 18 deals in serious play right now and I know that half of them are going to fall through. I won't get the price I want; there will be a title problem or a money problem or some kind of problem. I don't own them yet, but they're in play. Most investors have only one in play and they beat it to death. They follow it through and their fallout rate is 100 percent. Do sports teams go out and play only one game all year? No. Nor should real estate investors. Make lots of offers, do the numbers, and stick with it.

Research Property Values

One of my students, George, went out and found 42 town houses. He found out the seller wanted $46,000 for every town house, or $1.9 million for the 42 units.

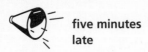
five minutes late

Investing is highly competitive. There's a big investor in my town named Hal who helped me get started in real estate. Hal finds deals and sells them to me; sometimes I find deals and sell them to him. We exchange information. I call him and say, "Hal, what's this neighborhood all about? What are these properties worth? What about those apartments over there?" Like Hal, investors in your town can be of great help to you. They know the markets, and they are buyers and sellers. Get to know them.

One time, I went to a deal and arrived five minutes before Hal. In those five minutes, I got a signed contract. For about 30 seconds, Hall was upset for being late, and then he said, "Well, I've got to go. I'm looking at another deal today."

If you're in real estate, you have more deals and things to look at than you have time.

Because the homes were in Maryland and neither George nor I knew real estate values there, I called an investor in my network who knows the neighborhood and asked, "What are 42 town houses in this part of Maryland worth?" He learned that they rented for about $700 a month and that investors pay $50,000 for those kind of town homes, though they are worth about $59,000 each. Knowing that, George offered $43,000 a unit, which would give him $3,000 profit each. He pockets a total of $126,000 for making some phone calls, finding a motivated seller, and putting the seller and buyer together.

Get That Contract Signed

Have you ever looked at a deal and said, "Gee, this is great! They're going to sell this house for $200,000 and I can sell it for $250,000. I'm going to make $50,000 and I know it's going to work. I've been over there 20 times. I've talked to them; it's going to be great." But after a week, you call the real estate agent and learn that somebody else put in a contract. You procrastinated and now it's gone.

Until you have a signed contract, you have nothing but dreams, so get that signed contract. As the old proverb says, "He who hesitates is lost." I cover contracts in greater depth in Chapter 11.

Build Three Databases

Real estate is like almost any other business. Your income and wealth will be related to the activity you do and the people you know. Every business, especially real estate, is a people business.

To make deals happen without using your own money, you need just three simple databases, and you build them on a daily basis. Every time you talk to a Realtor, respond to an ad, or meet anyone in any situation, take time to find out which of the following three categories that person might fit into; as you make calls and talk to people, add their information to your databases:

1. Potential motivated sellers

2. Potential buyers

3. Sources of money

Here are some examples: "Oh you're a Realtor? Do you know of any good mortgage companies that lend money, or work with investors, or help first-time home buyers?" Perhaps you are calling on For Rent ads in the paper to find a motivated seller. You might ask, "You're an older landlord or landlady who's bought and sold a lot of properties. Do you

robert's tip

I once responded to a newspaper ad (in the investment property section of a local newspaper) about an investment house for sale. It was worth about $90,000, and the owner sold it to me for $65,000 on owner's terms, with nothing down. I turned around and sold it to someone else for $10,000 down, with the buyer taking over the mortgage payments. I made about $100 a month for many, many years on this deal in addition to the $10,000 up-front profit.

When I went to the closing, I was feeling extremely happy. I had this great deal after being in the business only three years. For the first time, I asked the older gentleman, "By the way, do you have—or know of anyone who has—more properties for sale?" He said, "I'm so glad you asked. I've got 88 more." I wholesaled, or flipped, about 50 of his 88 properties and made a lot of money.

So remember this. If you're talking to an investor, landlord, or real estate agent, ask this question *every time:* "Do you have more properties?"

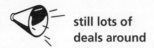

still lots of deals around

Sometimes I am interviewed on radio talk shows, and callers tell me there are no deals left to be found. One caller had reviewed my book, *Unlimited Riches,* and decided I was out of my mind, saying, "Robert, you can't buy houses 20 to 30 percent below what they're worth." I explained that during the time that book was being written, I'd bought a $500,000 condo for $258,000. That was about 50 cents on the dollar. Maybe I should have said, "Yes, I am having trouble finding 20 and 30 percent below-market-value deals—because sometimes I'm getting 50 percent ones."

want to lend money on real estate and make a 9, 10, or 11 percent return on your money?" If such people have funds to lend, you could borrow from them or they could become your money partners. Remember, you're always looking for potential deals, potential buyers, and potential sources of funding.

Within a few weeks of doing this, you'll have 10 or 20 names, addresses, phone numbers, fax numbers, and e-mail addresses in all three of those categories. Congratulations, you're now in business. Most investors calling on a For Sale ad are looking for a deal; if they don't sniff a deal, they hang up the phone. But you're looking for much more than deals—you want potential buyers and sources of funding, too. You're building a network of buyers, sellers, suppliers, and financiers.

Understand Profit Margins

Profit margins on wholesale, or flip, deals will be different from each other, depending on the type of property, how well you negotiate, what deals you find, and the area you are in. Generally, on a single-family home, you ought to get the property for 20 to 30 percent below its market value. If a house is worth $100,000, you should get it under contract for $70,000 and make anywhere from $5,000 to $15,000 for wholesaling it. Then, when you flip it to someone else for $85,000 who fixes it up and sells it, he or she makes $15,000 on a $100,000 house.

I suggest making at least 10 percent of the gross, so if it's $400,000 you should make $40,000. Put it under contract for $280,000, sell it to someone for $320,000. Of course, each deal is different and your results may vary.

CLOSING ON A FLIPPED PROPERTY

There are several ways to close on a property that's been flipped, and four of them are described here: collapsed closing, one closing, assigning the contract, and putting the property under option.

Collapsed Closing

Here's how a *collapsed closing* works. You're buying a property for $200,000 and the lawyer deeds the property from the seller to you. At the same moment, there is a deed and a closing statement from you to the end buyer. The buyer comes in at 3:00 P.M. with mortgage money of $250,000. The funds are wired in or the buyer has a cashier's check and gives it to the attorney. The attorney takes the money and finishes the paperwork, then goes to the next room at 3:30 P.M. and gives the seller $200,000, pays off the liens, does the closing. A deed passes from the seller to you and from you to the buyer. The seller doesn't care what the deed says. He or she is interested in getting his $200,000. And you get $50,000 for being in the middle.

Wait a minute. We've got a problem. The seller paid all the closing costs of $2,000 for one transaction, and the buyer paid all the closing costs of $2,000 for the other transaction. Any excess closing funds should go to you, but you left out a statement to ensure that in your contracts. So the closing attorney has to follow contract law, stating there are two deeds and only one title insurance and there is double money here— another $2,000. What do you tell the lawyer to do with it? Read the contract. You just made $2,000.

One Closing

The other standard way is called *one closing*. There is one deed from the original seller to the end buyer; you are not in the deed. (That's preferable because mortgage companies don't endorse a property going from one person to another person in a day or a week.) The deed goes from the seller for $200,000 to the buyer for $250,000, and you get the difference. There is one closing statement, and you get a finder's fee.

Some mortgage companies don't like a middle person; they want the property to go from one person to the other without a flip fee. The process can be subject to fraud. Instead of getting a flip fee, call it a finder's fee, consulting fee, marketing fee, or some other fee that comes off the back of the closing statement similar to liens, taxes, attorney's fees, title fees, and survey fees listed in the closing statement. Now it says that a $50,000 fee, to you or your company name, is for finding the deal.

If that doesn't work, you can get the original seller to sign a debt and put a lien on the property for $50,000. The lien has to be paid off in order to pass title to the end buyer, so your finder's fee becomes a lien and comes off the back of the closing statement. Banks and mortgage companies generally don't care what comes off the back. But they don't want to see you buy a property for $150,000, which then goes to me for $200,000, and finally to a third party for $250,000, all within a short period of time. Instead, do a collapsed closing and take it as a fee or a lien off the back of the closing statement. Let your attorney help you out with that; that is how you get paid.

Assign the Contract

A better way to flip properties is to *assign your contract.* You have a contract to buy it from the seller for $200,000, and the buyer is willing to pay you $250,000, so have the buyer purchase your contract and you get $50,000. The wording says, "I assign this contract, the right to buy the house for $200,000, to you." Have you ever heard of the option market in stocks? There isn't any liability involved; the buyer simply bought your contract, just as people buy and sell the right to buy and sell the stocks. About a billion of them go around a day. You can do it with real estate.

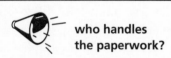
who handles the paperwork?

I always get a real estate attorney involved because if there's a mistake, that person is on the hook, not me. A lot of investors and seminars suggest you do your own paperwork, saying, "Here's a copy of this form; just fill it in; it's so easy." But I never do it because I don't do legal documents every day. What if I miss a sentence, or what if a new law was passed a month ago? I want to work with an attorney who does this kind of paperwork every day.

Put the House under Option

One of my students never signs a contract to buy property; he thinks it's risky. He does between a half million and $1 million a year flipping properties by working the courthouse angle: He finds all the estate sales, probates, and foreclosures and puts them under contract and flips them. He has never owned a property, never hired a contractor, never borrowed any money. He's been doing this for six years. He simply flips, flips, flips.

His preference is to *put the properties under option*. The contract states, "I'll give you $10 for the right to buy the house for $200,000; I option it." That means he sells the option to the end buyer and lets the title company close it. If he doesn't end up buying that property, all he loses is $10.

You could make a fortune just doing options. For example, you option to buy a hotel for $10 million and then find someone who will pay $11 million and buy your option. You step out of it at the closing gong.

PROS AND CONS OF WHOLESALING

The good news about wholesaling is that it's fun; if you do it right, you really have little risk and you don't need any capital. You may need a little earnest money every now and then, but you don't really need serious money to start. Also, it's profitable.

Now here's the bad news. When you flip something, you make a nice profit, then you've got to flip something else; you've got to keep doing it, like sales. If you don't sell something next week, you don't get paid (unless you have set up some source of residual income).

Another disadvantage about wholesaling properties is taxes. If you buy and sell chairs and make a profit, you have to pay your normal income tax rate on whatever you make after all the expenses, plus you have to pay a self-employment tax, which is about 14 to 16 percent of what you make. When you work for a company, the company takes half of the taxes out of your paycheck and you pay the other half. So the government is going to get its 14 or 16 percent whether you work for somebody else or whether you work for yourself.

If you buy property (or anything else) with the intention of selling it for a profit, you're self-employed and charged a self-employment tax above and beyond your income tax. The way to reduce some of that is to write off everything you legally and ethically can so that on paper you can show less income and thus are taxed on less. Of course, for this, call on one of the most important members of your support team—your tax accountant.

FOUR STEPS TO WHOLESALE PROFITS

I hope I've convinced you to delve into this low-risk, low-capital strategy of investing in real estate. All it takes are four simple steps: (1) Find a good deal; (2) get it under contract; (3) find a buyer for it; (4) close the sale.

chapter 8

lease options: the real estate investor's best-kept secret

People are moved and motivated by emotions. Living is a constant process of trying to satisfy emotional needs and wants.

—Robert Conklin

If you rent a house or an apartment for $1,000 a month, what do you have at the end of the year? Well, $12,000 worth of canceled checks, right? Zip, zilch, zero. Everyone can use lease optioning. Even if you don't make a lot of money or don't choose to be a real estate investor, you can do one on your own house and stop throwing away your rent dollars. Would you like a vacation home? A house in the mountains or condo by the beach? You have a choice. You can pay $200,000, but what if after a year or two you don't like the place or you want to go somewhere else? You're stuck because you bought it. You might have to sell it, and what if the market has gone down? However, you could lease-option a vacation home. Stop throwing your rent dollars away, *and* stop using your own money to buy property.

Let's talk about cars for a minute. There used to be only two ways to buy a car. One way was cash: If you wanted the Camaro with the mag wheels and the flared fenders, and it cost $12,000, you could pay $12,000 in cash. Alternatively, you could borrow $12,000 from the car company or the bank if they'd lend you the money, but your payments would be high.

Today, about half of all cars are sold using a lease with an option to buy. You can get the new BMW for $42,000, or put $499 down and pay just $399 a month. People don't care about total price; they are more interested in the down payment and monthly outlay. We get excited when we see we can drive a Porsche for $2,000 down option money and $599 a month, because we tend to think of a $90,000 Porsche as unaffordable. Now, all of a sudden, it is affordable.

Some wise businesspeople figured out they could lease-option cars. That means you drive it for two or three years and, if you like it and want to keep it, pay it off at a reduced price because some of your payments have already gone toward buying the car. It's a win-win situation. If you don't want to keep the car, you simply return it. Lease optioning offers the best of all worlds. Indeed, a whole industry has emerged out of this concept.

Well, I'm sorry to say that in your town, likely less than 0.02 of 1 percent of houses and condominiums are lease-option deals. Why? Because you haven't gone out there and done it yet. I've never seen more than 10 ads for lease-option houses in any big city, so you can create this in your own city. I also believe it's the answer to the problems associated with low-income housing, as it will definitely help poor people buy homes.

A WALK THROUGH A LEASE-OPTION DEAL

How do you find good lease-option deals? What's the best source? Look under Properties for Rent in the local newspaper. Every landlord or landlady who is renting properties has major complaints. They say, "Tenants bug me; repairs, repairs, repairs; it's a lot of work; there are lots of headaches." They rent properties for $1,000 a month but never *make* $1,000 a month because they've got to spend a lot of time and money fixing them up. They might be empty right now because the last tenants ran out on them. It's frustrating. Anyone in the landlord business has plenty of problems, headaches, and repair expenses.

If you could get them out of the repair business—and could ensure

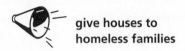 **give houses to
homeless families**

Consider a single mom who's been living in a shelter and can't qualify to rent anything. Her credit is wrecked; she's been homeless for a long while. Who wants to rent to someone with no current address and no income, whose credit scores are horrible, and who has had a job for only a short time?

Every year I go to a shelter and choose a single mom who has a job. She has no credit, no down payment, and can't rent anything. I find a house that's worth about $75,000. I buy it for $45,000 and put in a few thousand dollars worth of repairs. I borrow the $45,000; my payment on that loan is $350 a month. On the open market, the rent on that $75,000 house would be $700, but she couldn't afford that much rent even if someone over-looked her credit history.

Here's my strategy. I offer to rent it to her for $400 a month, which covers my loan payment. I also give her an option to buy it. She can buy it from me at my cost of $45,000. (I could also option it to her at $50,000 or $55,000 if I wanted to make a little money.) She pays the $400 a month, which I use to make the payment and escrow the remaining $50. At the end of the year, she's got $600 in savings. If people with bad credit pay all of their bills on time for one year, their credit rating goes to a B– or B+ score. That's not perfect (A or A+ would be perfect), but it's good enough to get an 80 to 90 percent loan to value in most cases.

There are programs in which the city and state banks want low-income people to buy homes and so will grant part of the money. Some programs create home ownership by training people how to become homeowners in free workshops, which I have the single mom attend. We have a written agreement that she has to keep a job, not incur any more debt, and pay her bills on time. We also show her how to start repairing her credit. In one year, she can buy the house that's worth $75,000 for $45,000 or $55,000. When she buys that house for $55,000, her payment will be about $400 a month for a 30-year loan at 6 to 8 percent interest. (She'll actually need a little more for taxes and insurance.) Now you see how you can make money and simultaneously offer good lease options to homeless people.

that they receive their checks on time every month so they can go on vacation—would they be interested in talking with you? Definitely.

Start by asking questions. How long have they had the property? How's the rental going? What do they rent it for? What have the repairs cost over the years? If you found the landlord through a For Rent ad, then the property is empty. If so, you'd ask these questions: How long has it been empty? One month? Two months? Three months? Last year, how often was it empty? What were the repairs? Have they enjoyed being a landlord or landlady or manager? Have they had any problems? What don't they like about it? What would they change about it?

Then work the numbers for the landlords you talk with and show them a solution in writing. For example, if they rent a property for $1,000 a month but it's been empty for two months, that means they're not collecting the full $1,000—they're really collecting about $700 prorated over the year. How much did they spend on maintenance and repairs? Say they spent $1,000 cleaning it and painting it. That means they're not making even $700 a month; they're making only $600 a month.

Work the numbers backward, both annually and monthly, for the past two or three years. Then ask them how much time they spend working on or worrying about the property. They might say about four hours a month—they had to drive over there and fix the commode. Is their time worth $10 an hour, $30 an hour, $50 an hour? Now the income isn't even $600 a month; it's $500 a month. Show them that, with all the work, all the headaches, all the problems, all the bills, they're really making only $500 a month as landlords.

Work the numbers. Say that landlord is making only $500 a month, and the market rent is about $1,000 (which you verified by calling some other property managers and landlords). Ask this question: "Mr. Landlord, if I could get you out of the repair business and get your money to you every time, what's the least amount you'd take per month?"

"Well, I rent it for $1,000, but it's clear I'm making a lot less than that."

 **think about it**

You might call some landlords and be told the units are always rented, they've always collected the money owed, and there have been no repairs. If that's the case, they are not likely telling the truth. But if that's what they say, then they don't have a problem you can fix. Move on. Follow the other For Rent ads in your newspaper and For Rent signs in your neighborhood for houses, duplexes, condominiums, commercial properties, shopping centers, and office buildings. You can lease-option any kind of property. Just pick what you like.

Okay, you negotiate, negotiate, negotiate. (You'll learn how to do this in Chapter 10.) Let Mr. Landlord speak first, but mentally know your ceiling price—the top price you're willing to offer. Maybe it's $650, maybe even $700, because you know you can rent it for at least $1,000.

Let's say your negotiations are weak and he insists on $700, that's it. You lease it from him for five years for $700 a month. That effectively locks in the rent amount for five years, too. Maybe you can lock it in for 10 years, even 20 years.

Now ask the least amount he'd take to sell this property, because you'd like to make an offer to buy it. Let's say you think the house is worth $100,000 and he responds to that question by saying, "I just had an appraisal. It's worth about $100,000." Because you're both investors, he might say, "I know you're going to make a lot of money, I'll sell it to you for $88,500." Well, that's not a good deal; it's a bad deal because it's only 12 percent below what it's worth.

This *could* be a dangerous deal, but let me show you why it may not be such a bad deal. You could continue the negotiations by saying, "Mr. Landlord, if I pay you $700 a month, give me $150 a month credit toward the purchase price. That way, every month you make a payment, you get a bit of equity buildup or debt payoff, just as you would if you had bought it and borrowed the money." Also remind him how much the little repairs drove him crazy—the broken sinks and commodes and all that (which tend to be 70 or 80 percent of the repairs). You'll take responsibility for those repairs off his shoulders; the landlord will still be responsible for the big repairs, anything over $500 or maybe $1,000 or maybe $300—whatever you can negotiate.

In cases like this, landlords will ask for money down. Every property needs repairs, so let's say there are $3,000 worth of repairs. We'll get that taken care of, so instead of giving them $3,000 option money, you'll do the repairs. Who's really going to do the repairs? Your end buyer, not you; you are out of the repair business. You've gotten a landlord out of the small-repairs business. You have a five-year option to buy the property for $88,000, and it's worth $100,000. Horrible deal, $150 a month credit. Protect yourself: The question in your mind is, what if I can't rent this or sell it quickly? You're stuck. The property is currently empty, so negotiate delaying the first payment for 90 days or 100 days. What if they don't go for that? Try 60 days. What if they don't go for that? Try 30 days. Make a business decision.

I've said it before, but it bears repeating here: Disclose everything you do in writing. Tell them you're a real estate investor—that you don't represent them or their interests, that this offer is based on your being able to remarket the property in the next 60 or 90 days. If you can't rent it in 60 days because the market is terrible and the house is horrible and you made a big mistake, you walk away. They're not any worse off, it's empty anyway—they're not making any money. Not everyone will agree to that disclaimer or contingency, but you'll get it most of the time if you ask properly.

Let's say you have 60 days. They signed a lease for five years at $700 a month, giving $150 a month credit, and you also have an option to buy it for $88,000 within the next five years, with some of the rent going to knock down that purchase price. How much money do you put down? Zero. How much money have you borrowed? Zero. How many contractors have you hired? Zero.

Clean up the yard and give the house a coat of paint to make it marketable. Then run an ad in the paper: "Easy qualifying, become a homeowner, stop throwing your rent dollars away, no banks involved, won't last." Create a sense of urgency. Have a voice mail people can call that describes all the attributes of the house. You think the house is worth $100,000. You think the market rent is $1,000 because you've done research—gotten comps and verified figures with property managers. Your phone might ring off the hook because now you can sell a house with easy qualifying.

The first responders call and say they'd like to buy this house; they're familiar with the neighborhood. The number one qualifying question to ask a potential lease-option candidate is this: "How much money do you have to put down?" Ask additional questions like these: "Do you have anything to sell? Any tax refunds coming? Any other sources of funds?" People often don't think about some of these things. Tell them you might get back to them and put their information in a file.

The second responders call and say they're looking to buy a house, but they don't think they can qualify. They don't have a big down payment, they have only $6,000. You can screen them over the phone.

Do a credit and criminal background check on everybody. Also screen them by sending them to your mortgage company and getting them prequalified. Explain how your home-ownership program works:

They don't have to have perfect credit. They don't have to have a big down payment. But you need to check them out. Sometimes the mortgage company calls back and says your candidates are prequalified. Say the mortgage company has a 95 percent loan program for them, and they have enough of a down payment to proceed.

How much are you selling the house for? You thought it was worth $100,000. What's the actual difference if they pay $105,000 or $109,000 for 30 years at 7 percent? About $8 or $10 a month. So you write a contract for $107,000, in which they pay all the closing costs and fork over $6,000 as a down payment. They're happy. They didn't think they could buy a home, and you showed them how. Now you're ready to close.

Call the original seller. He wanted $88,000 but you can renegotiate that amount. As of now, $107,000 minus $88,000 means $19,000 profit in your pocket. And you already have $6,000 in option money. So you've received $6,000 plus $19,000 and you'll make another $13,000 at closing.

How would you like some extra money? Call up the original sellers and say, "Hey, I have five years." Always count it out, 2004, 2005, 2006, 2007, 2008. You'll give them $88,000 in five years; however, you're paying off some of the loan as you go, so it won't even be that much. Ask this question: "Would you like the money sooner?" They might say yes. If they receive the cash in the next 30 days, they tell you, they'd take a vacation, pay off bills, and so on. Great. Next ask them, "If you get that cold hard cash in your hands in the next 30 days, what's the least amount you'd take?" If they say $87,000, what do you say then? "Can you do any better?" If not, you agree to $87,000. You go to closing and sell it for $107,000. You just made $20,000 on a bad deal that you put no money into because you learned how to lease-option and do credit financing. You learned how to hustle, market, and take action.

RELATED ITEMS

They put down $6,000 option money. Whose pocket does that go into? Yours. You don't pay taxes on it until it closes or the lease buyers walk away from it. Hold onto it, because you may need that money to help close if they buy the house.

Second thing, your note to the original seller is $700 a month. You know the market rent is $1,000, but first ask these people the magic question: How much are they looking to spend per month? Well, they don't want to spend more than $1,100. You just got a $100 rent increase. They pay $1,100, and because you're a nice person, you give them $200 a month credit toward the purchase price every month, so they're not just throwing their rent dollars away. What's $1,100 minus $700 a month? $400 a month in your pocket if they continue to rent and not buy it.

- How long is their lease option? One-year lease, one-year option.
- They are responsible for the first $500 of repairs.
- Preapprove them. Do credit and criminal background checks. Get at least two landlord references from them.

Why two landlord references? If they're currently renting from Bill the landlord and they're bad tenants (e.g., drug dealers, don't pay the rent, tear the property up), what might Bill say? "Oh, they're great, man, I'm going to help move them over tomorrow. I'm loading their truck right now." But if they rented from Sue two years ago and didn't pay the rent, dealt drugs, tore up everything, Sue is likely to tell the truth because they no longer live in her property: "They don't pay the rent. They deal drugs. Don't rent to them."

Get the Option Money Up Front

What's the worst thing that can happen? Number one, six months go by, they don't pay the rent, trash the house, and they leave town. You have $6,000 in option money to do the repairs. It might take you $2,000 to $3,000 to paint the place and clean it up, so you make $3,000 profit, then lease-option it to somebody else, who puts $8,000 down and pays $1,200 a month.

Number two, most people don't lease-option their property because someone actually might buy it. A lot of landlords won't lease-option their rental property because, if someone actually buys it, they won't have it anymore. Get the money and go find another deal, right? I could sell all my property today and in three months I'd have better deals. So could you if you learn how to do this and get busy.

What's the third worst thing that could happen? A year goes by, they made the payments, and they leave. Great. Not a problem. You lease-option it again. Your debt goes down, you keep their option money, and they move on.

Clarify the Terms of Your Lease Option

If they miss a rent payment or are late by one day, they lose all their option money. If you rent out an apartment, what's the tenants' incentive to pay on time? Not much. If they're late, they pay a measly little late fee.

What's the number one complaint all landlords have against renters? They damage the place and don't take care of it. Are you shocked? Have you ever rented a car? You are no doubt nice, honest, and ethical. When you rent that car, how do you treat it? Do you drive over the bumps in the parking lot, take the curb, do some donuts? Let's floor it, see what this little rental car can really do, drink a Coke, throw it in the back seat, right? Don't we all tend to do the same? Why? It's not that we're bad; it's just that it's not ours.

When you lease-option, tell your tenants they're on a home-ownership program, that this is their house. They're going to fix it up. It's theirs. Way to go. They own it. They're buying it. They're lease-optioning it. They may plant some flowers, paint, maybe put a porch on the back. If they're homeowners, they take care of it.

- If they're late on the rent, they lose the option money.
- If they don't buy within a year, they lose the option money.

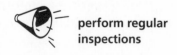 **perform regular
inspections**

How do you make sure that the property is not being destroyed and that your tenants are doing the repairs they are supposed to do? In every lease and lease option, you have the right to inspect the property every 30 days. I predetermine my inspection date in writing. For example, I say, "On the second Tuesday of every month, during business hours, I have the right to go in and inspect for repairs, check the air-conditioning filters, spray for bugs." Inspect it every 30 days; if you don't, you could be shocked at what you find.

- If they do any damage or don't do the repairs, they lose the option money.
- If they don't close on a new mortgage within a year, they lose the option money.

In my landlord course, I explain that all my rent is due on the first of the month, late on the fifth, and we evict on the eleventh. This is my policy and procedure. I promise you, if tenants can't pay this month's rent, they probably can't pay three months' rent if you let them stay in your rental property.

I believe if all contracts were handwritten, there wouldn't be lawsuits. "I didn't understand that I would lose the option money because it was in a big contract." Wait a minute, you have, in their own writing, "If I don't make my rent payment on time, I lose my option money." In all my lease options, I get the tenants to detail it in their own handwriting. If we go to court, the tenant-buyers cannot say that they didn't know about it, that they didn't understand, that it's too complicated. I get everyone to write in their own handwriting, "I understand that if I miss a payment, I will lose my option money. I understand if I don't do all the repairs, I will lose my option money. I understand that if I don't close on the house within a year with a new mortgage, I will lose my option money."

robert's tip

Include lease options as part of your overall real estate investment plan.

Say a month goes by and the tenant-buyer moves in, calls up, and says, "Oh my God, the commode is leaking, get over here and fix this thing." It happens all the time. We remind all our tenant-buyers about the lease option they signed. It says they're responsible for the first $500 in repairs and therefore they need to fix it themselves. They may say that's not fair, they don't remember that. We tell them we've got a copy of that agreement in the file; it's something they wrote in their own handwriting. They have a copy, too, but offer to read it to them, or ask if they want you to send them a copy. "Oh, ah, I kinda remember that." Having that paperwork will protect you. Make a point of getting them to write the agreement in their own handwriting.

If, after a year, they don't close on the house but they want to stay there, renegotiate the terms. Maybe get more option money or increase the rent. Real estate generally goes up, so if you control property for five years on a lease option, not only does the property value increase, but also the rent. How would you like to do lease options for 10 years? You lock in the price today for 10 years. Could you have made some money if you'd locked in 100 houses 10 years ago?

POLICIES AND PROCEDURES FOR LEASE OPTIONING

As a review of this important system of real estate investing, here are the guidelines for lease optioning, summarized:

1. Write separate lease and option contracts.

2. Include repair contingencies and make sure the lease buyers understand they're responsible for minor repairs.

3. Make sure you are a named insured on the property. If the property burns, for example, you will get nothing if you're not the named insured.

4. Whose name is the house in? The original owners. That's okay, because you don't have any liability, but you may want to have them transfer it into a land trust or into your name.

5. Always ask for the deed; if you don't get the deed, lease-option it.

6. Record at the courthouse that you have an option on the property. Run your numbers and verify that your values and rents are correct, because you always want more money coming in than going out.

7. Do a title search to be certain that the person you are negotiating with is the decision maker and owner.

8. Confirm that the property taxes have been paid.

9. Run ads. Keep a constant stream of tenant-buyers. Screen, screen, screen them, and have them preapproved for financing.

part III

expanding your knowledge base

learning to evaluate and analyze every detail in 90 minutes or less

A prudent question is one-half of wisdom.
—Francis Bacon

Do you analyze a property for buying, for selling, or for renting? Yes—for any property. You need to make an analysis with any sale. More important, you need to build in a margin for error. Determine how much money is coming in and going out, but do not buy strictly based on cash flow. You still need to buy a property for less than what it is worth today, so you have room to sell it when you want to.

In addition to margin of error, be aware of the property's finance-ability. The bigger the deals you chase, the more difficult it may be at certain times to get financing. You might have to put what I call *real* (that is, your own) money into it. In fact, on large commercial or investment deals, lenders may insist you put in some of your own cash.

ANALYSIS PARALYSIS

One of the biggest stumbling blocks of successful investing (and this applies to me, too) is called *paralysis of analysis.* You stumble into a good deal and then you stop dead in your tracks. You think about purchasing, worry about the decision, and *never do* anything.

In my first six months of real estate investing, I looked at hundreds of great deals and I did nothing. How did I know it was a good deal? How did I know I could make money? I was scared to death to make an offer because if I did, I might have actually gotten the deal. Then what?

As we learned earlier, a great deal in real estate is something you can really make money on. There are two approaches to making money in real estate: (1) speculation and (2) investing.

With real estate *speculation,* you buy property that is priced near market value, or put it under contract. For example, you buy something worth half a million dollars for $499,000 and pray that it quickly goes up in value to $550,000 or $600,000.

With real estate *investing,* you look for something you can either put under contract or buy for 20 to 40 percent lower than what it is really worth. That means a property worth $500,000 today would be put under contract for $400,000 or less to make it worthwhile. Face it, if you had to sell this property for $475,000, you would still come out okay because you had a 20 percent margin of error in this deal.

To protect your income source and overcome any analysis paralysis, (1) make sure you have a good deal (because even if it is not as good as you think, you still have a margin of error to work with), and (2) get lots

---

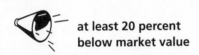 **at least 20 percent
below market value**

Rule of thumb: Do not buy property that is not at least 20 or 25 percent below what you really think it is worth today in its current condition. I am not talking about a property worth $100,000 that needs $20,000 worth of work and sells for $80,000. I am talking about having it at least 20 to 25 percent below what it is really worth in today's market.

If you look at enough deals, you will find some well below the value of comparable properties. If you never look and analyze deals, you will not find any.

of information. If I said, "Let me tell you the exact cards that will come out on the blackjack table: Without a doubt, your next hand will be a 19 and the dealer will have 18. The next one, you are going to have 21 and the dealer 18," you would be inclined to play because you would have information about what will happen. This can also happen in real estate investing when you gather lots of meaningful information.

ANALYZE IN LESS THAN 90 MINUTES

To analyze any property deal in less than 90 minutes and not get bogged down in analysis paralysis, find the answers to these three questions:

1. What is the property worth today?

2. What repairs are needed, and how much will they cost? (Most properties, even brand-new homes, need repairs.)

3. What can you get it for?

What Is the Property Worth Today?

Remember, to develop a successful real estate investing career, your job is to find deals and put them together. Your job is *not* to become an appraiser, a closing attorney, a management expert, or a repair person. Use professionals!

Say we parachute you into Naples, Florida. You have never been there before and your goal is to find good deals. What would you do? As discussed in Chapter 5, you look at newspaper ads, drive for dollars, call For Rent ads, For Sale ads, and so on. You are certain to find prospects that may become suspects, so you call one of the property owners, who says, "I think the building is worth $100,000. I will let you have it for $50,000 and it needs very few repairs." But you do not know if it is really worth $100,000. So you call a Realtor who sells a lot of property in that area and ask, "A three-bedroom, two-bath on Apple Street in Naples, Florida—what would it sell for?" He replies, "I've sold two in the last month, one for $99,000, the other for $102,500." You just learned that house is worth about $100,000.

Still, it is important to call two or three people to verify the information you get. Another Realtor might say, "Nothing has sold there in a year. The last offer we got was for $79,900."

If you are looking for commercial property, call a commercial broker or an appraiser and ask, "What would something similar to this property bring in today's market?" Follow up by getting a list of comparable sales in that area from real estate professionals.

How do Realtors, appraisers, and banks determine what a property is worth? They look at comparable sales, usually three to five sales of very similar property close by. Realize that you cannot compare three bedrooms with eight bedrooms; you cannot compare 2-story office buildings with 30-story office buildings. The properties have to be similar.

Take it a step further and get a list of comparable sales. You can actually find lists on the Internet (www.shemin.com) and see the sales price of every property bought or sold (and when it sold) for the street you want information about. In addition, talk with active professionals and ask, "What is the market like?" Then get the information in writing via fax, e-mail, or letter. Put comparable sales lists and information in a folder for future reference. (Remember, you cannot keep hounding Realtors and never do business with them, so get them to help you and let them have part of the commission.)

After you have done this 15 times in Naples, Florida, you will know the comparables by heart and have rapport with several Realtors.

What Repairs Does It Need?

If you have motivated sellers but their properties need repair, you can find the cost of the repairs from two different sources: from the owner or the seller (most are truthful; a few are not) and from a good contractor who is licensed, bonded, and referred to you. The most important word I just used is *referred*. Make sure you get bids from more than one contractor who comes recommended by respected Realtors or other investors. (Again, you cannot just get bids all the time from contractors and never work with them. Likely you will close on some deals, get repairs done, and give the contractor glowing references. If that does not happen in a timely way, pay the contractors for their written bids.)

What Can You Get It For?

When sellers are motivated to move a property worth $100,000 and it does not need any repairs, they may say, "We'll let you have it for $70,000." (Thirty percent below market value.) Would that be a good deal? Yes. So negotiate an even better deal and get a signed contract. That is where you make your money in real estate.

Before you had access to this book, you may have gotten excited and said, "Oh my God, it's worth $100,000 and it's being offered to me for $70,000! I'm going to sign the contract right now." You would have made some money on this deal, but you would have also made a grave error. By not negotiating, you may have potentially left a lot of money on the table.

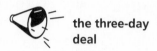

the three-day deal

When I was asked to be a guest on *The Leeza Gibbons Show* (a TV talk show), Leeza Gibbons challenged me to find a good real estate deal in Los Angeles, California. The producers knew I was from Tennessee and did not know the L.A. real estate market. They also knew I liked to give away homes to homeless people, so they said, "Come out to Los Angeles. If you find a good deal, then you can give a house to a homeless family right on our show." They gave me only three days to put a good deal together.

On my first day, I decided to follow my own advice and drive for dollars in a particular area. I was driving around at six in the morning. When people wearing bathrobes came out of their houses to get their newspapers, I asked them, "What do these houses sell for? I'm looking for a place in this neighborhood." I quickly learned that the worst, cheapest houses in the worst neighborhood started at about $120,000. A little different from Tennessee values. Next, I chased down some For Sale signs and made some calls. After two days, I found three bank foreclosures, one landlord, and four great deals. The best one was a two-bedroom condominium with a pool and tennis court. It was appraised for well over $140,000, and I put it under contract for $42,000 with terms from the bank.

How did I determine what real estate values were in that neighborhood? I asked everybody I met, including Realtors, "What are these houses selling for?"

I also needed information about repairs, so a contractor (referred, of course) gave me a written bid for $3,500 to get this condo in tip-top shape.

Third, I negotiated. The bank that was foreclosing on the condo wanted $42,000 to satisfy the loan. I was able to take it over on a short sale because of my good credit. Now this bank can show this as a good loan on their books instead of a bad one.

Then I called back the producers of *Leeza*. At first, they refused to believe me, declaring, "Nothing in Los Angeles sells for under $100,000. You must be making up stories." I had to show them all the paperwork and they finally believed me. We gave that condo to a homeless family right on the show.

short selling

When a bank takes back a property because a loan went bad, often it discounts the property for the amount of the loan. This is referred to as a *short sale* or *short selling*.

Every property's value is in the eyes of its beholder. If you own a lot of real estate and you are being sued, you might make a case that your property is not worth much and needs repairs. On the other hand, if you go to the bank to borrow as much money as you can against the property, you will want it appraised as high as possible using the highest comparable sales. And when the tax assessor calls to figure out your new taxes for next year, you will say the rents are low, the buildings need work, and so on. Since property has different value depending on who is looking at it, make sure you talk to professionals active in the market who tell you honestly what buyers are paying for their properties today.

The best way to determine market value is by attracting an offer through a newspaper ad that includes details of the property. See if the phone rings. Likewise, if you want to see how much rent should be, run a For Rent ad and see if anybody calls. If no one calls, you may not have much of a market.

Put It under Contract

You have negotiated a good price and *put it under contract* with the contingency clause. Now *do your analysis.* Beginners have a tendency to analyze for six weeks before putting in an offer. But by the time they find out the age of the hot water heater and the condition of the roof shingles, and have talked to the neighbors five times, their opportunity may have disappeared.

Instead, at the beginning, do a quick survey to see if it is a good deal, document everything, put your offer in with a contingency, and then do your analysis or due diligence. Remember, if you wait too long, you will lose a lot of deals.

Get Appraisals

Remember, you can always spend a few hundred dollars and get an appraisal done on a property. You may even get the seller to pay for all or part of it. Have a professional appraiser look at it, research comparable sales, and tell you its value. Sometimes when I go to a lender to finance a property, I have the appraisal in hand and can say, "Here's proof. It's worth $200,000. Can I borrow some money, please?"

Inspect the Property

You want an inspector who is experienced and familiar with repairs to do an inspection of the property. I generally use a licensed, referred, bonded contractor who can make sure the property meets codes and can identify major problems. Also, before closing on any property, I have it inspected for termites.

Get a Clear Title

Make sure you ask the seller, "Do you have clear title to this property?" Sometimes, when you deal with highly motivated sellers, you find out they do not have titles to the properties. They are handling a deal for their uncle, brother, sister, and so on. Either that or they have 22 liens against the property they forgot to tell you about.

Be sure to ask these questions:

- Do you have clear title?
- Are there any loans, liens, or judgments against the property?
- Is there more than one mortgage?

Again, verify everything in writing. And before closing, have an escrow agent do a title search and provide title insurance.

Crunch the Numbers

Real estate investing is real estate by the numbers. You want to know what the profit and loss on a property would be if someone were to buy it, fix it up, and sell it, or if someone should buy it and rent it. Answer all tax, insurance, rental rate, and expense questions. Document all the details so you are an informed buyer. Do this for any property, whether you are going to keep it, wholesale it, lease-option it, or finance it. You want to make sure it will provide cash flow for somebody, even if that somebody is not you.

Gather full details about the transaction costs for buying and selling the property: commission costs (if you work with a Realtor), recording fees (to record deeds), and all financial details that apply to the property, including the terms of any loan (total amount, balance owed, years to pay, interest rate, and so on).

ANALYSIS RECAP

When you talk to sellers, always, always, *always ask questions.* The most important questions are: Why are you selling? Why are you selling? Why are you selling? That will determine their motivation level. If sellers say, "I can take my time because I don't really need to sell," they are not motivated. But if they say, "We're moving out of state. Job transfer. Have to sell it in the next three weeks," or "We're going through a divorce," or "We're getting foreclosed on. We've got financial problems," they are most likely motivated.

Then ask, "What is the debt on the property?" If they owe $100,000, it is unlikely they will accept less than $100,000 (or whatever the debt is).

You want to ask, "What are the terms of the loan? What are the payments and interest rate? Are you current on the payments?" Almost every loan has a due-on-sale clause.

The next question is, "Do you have clear title? Whose name is the title in?"

**real estate
doctor**

What if you ask, "What is your mortgage? How much do you owe on the property?" and the seller says, "I'm not going to tell you. This is personal information."

Respond by saying, "I am a real estate doctor and want to help solve a problem. To be able to help you, like a doctor, I have to know your symptoms."

Always enter into the conversation with that intention. If you meet with resistance, say, "By the way, even if you don't want to tell me this information, it's all public information. It's on the Internet. It's at the Registrar of Deeds. I can call the courthouse, the tax assessor's office, and get it anyway. So please go ahead and help me help you. I'm a real estate doctor."

Also ask, "What are the mortgages? Are there additional mortgages, judgments, or liens? What repairs are needed?"

Concerning repairs, make a worksheet and write down the condition of:

- The roof
- The gutters
- The shingles
- The attic
- The ceiling
- The walls
- The electrical system
- The carpet
- The flooring
- The kitchen
- The windows
- The plumbing
- The basement
- The foundation
- The yard

Visualize the house from top to bottom. Ask what work needs to be done and how much it will cost. Then, if you are interested, put it under contract with a contingency and send over your contractor to verify in writing what was found. Get a detailed written bid from your contractor.

All of these items you look for are important to you if you have to finance the property, or sell it, or bring in a partner. Keep all of the details (comparable sales and the repair estimates) in your folder.

ACT LIKE THE BIG GUYS

By the way, this process reflects how most large commercial deals are handled with big companies involved. They use accountants, lawyers, and other professionals to make sure the numbers are accurate, then close on the deal. That is how you should manage your real estate business.

Most investors want to know everything up front before they put an offer in, but in reality, they do not have to. If you smell a good deal, put your offer in, and conduct your due diligence. However, make sure you have a good deal in hand, because if you put in a lot of offers and never close on them, no one will want to sign another one with you.

chapter 10

learning to negotiate: getting more of what you want and need from any deal

In a good negotiation, everybody wins something.
—Gerard Nierenberg

When I began in real estate, I found a house worth $80,000 and the owner said, "I'll sell it for $60,000." I thought it was a great deal (it would provide cash flow). I was so excited, I signed the contract immediately. I left a ton of money on the table, though, because I did not know I could negotiate. Over the years I learned these important negotiating lessons:

1. The first person who mentions a number loses.

2. Never mention a number until you *absolutely have to.*

3. Ask this magical question as many times as you can until they get upset: "Can you do any better?"

4. You cannot negotiate a good deal until you find out what the seller really needs.

To get great deals on property and buy them without using your own money, it only makes sense to learn how to negotiate well. Often you can negotiate a no-money-down deal if you are willing to learn how and apply it to many transactions (read more about this in the sidebar).

You can actually negotiate in all areas of a real estate transaction: price, terms, closing time, earnest money, contingencies, conditions. Negotiate for all of it. Most real estate investors and Realtors negotiate only on price. But I advise you to learn to negotiate in many areas, using

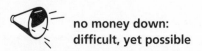

no money down: difficult, yet possible

Here are nine ways to buy property with little or no money down.

1. *Negotiate owner's terms with the seller.* Try (and *always* try) to have the seller sell you the property with no money down, with payments to be made monthly.

   Example: You find a home that you think is worth $75,000. You negotiate to buy it for $50,000, with zero cash at closing. The seller will pay all closing costs, and you pay $500 a month for 20 years. Sounds great, doesn't it? Well, *the seller would have to be pretty motivated to take a deal like this.* Nevertheless, I've seen it happen.

   If the house needs work, explain to the seller that you are going to spend time and money repairing the house—which is like a down payment. Your time and your money are going into the house so that the seller has little risk. In the event that you do not make payments to the seller, the seller gets to take back a home that is much more valuable because you just fixed it up.

   In negotiating owner's terms, always ask for the payments to begin as late as possible, with the first payment due in one year, in three months, or at the end of the first month. If you are buying to rent the house out, you can use the first month's rent to pay down your payments to the seller.

2. *Trade something you have of value.* This might be a car, a boat, tools. Barter anything you may have in place of a down payment. You never know what a seller might need.

3. *If the seller demands a down payment, ask the seller to agree to be paid on terms.* Example: Seller wants to sell for $100,000. You know it's a great deal, but you don't have the down payment. The seller insists on $10,000 down. Offer $11,000, but only if you can pay it over 30, 20, 10, or 5 years—or even 1 year.

(continued)

Continued

4. *Borrow money from another source for your down payment.* Example: credit lines, home equity lines, relatives, hard moneylenders, credit cards (careful), life insurance policies.

5. *Use the real estate agent's commission.* If the seller wants 6 percent to 10 percent down at closing, negotiate with the agent to take the commission over time. At the closing, the seller generally has to pay the commission in cash to the agent. If the agent agrees (you'll be surprised at the agent's flexibility) to take the commission in the form of a note, this saves the seller some cash at closing, which can go toward your down payment.

6. *Assume the seller's obligations.* Instead of making a cash down payment, assume some of the seller's notes and/or obligations. Perhaps the seller has a payment due; offer to make the payment yourself as your down payment.

7. *If you are buying a group of properties or land, sell off part of the land/properties for more than you have optioned or contracted for.* Then take the proceeds from that sale and make a down payment. Example: You are buying four houses for $30,000 per house. You know that they are worth more. You negotiate 60 days to close and you need 10 percent cash down to close. You flip one of the houses for $50,000 to someone else. At the simultaneous closing, you make your down payment from the $20,000 proceeds you just received on the flip. Yes, it can be done!

8. *Partner a deal.* If you find a property that is a great deal and you need 10 percent down to close (which you do not have), persuade a friend or an investor to partner with you. If your partner puts 10 percent down on the property, offer to split the profits 50-50 when you flip the house.

   Example: You find an apartment building that is worth $250,000 for sale at $150,000. The seller wants 10 percent down and will carry a note for 20 years at 10 percent interest (approximate payments of $1,300 per month). The apartment building has 10 units, and each one will rent, on average, for about $450 per month (or $4,500 per month total). You can make $3,200 per month (before expenses, of course)! But you don't have the down payment. Tell a friend or an investor about the deal—ask for the $15,000 down payment and offer your friend a 50 percent partnership on the deal. In 10 months' time, your partner will recoup his or her down payment, and you'll be making $1,600 per month and building equity. And you didn't even put up a dime!

9. *If you can get a line of credit from the bank, use it to purchase property.* Use the equity in your home to obtain a down payment. You'll be able to pay off the down payment over time at a reasonable rate, and you'll have an interest reduction on your taxes.

robert's tip

Go out in the next 24 hours and negotiate for something. Remember, negotiate only with the decision maker. When you're at a restaurant, for example, ask for the manager and build rapport by chatting and starting a dialogue like this:

"How long have you been working here?"

"I've been working here two years," the manager says.

"What a great restaurant; Cindy the waitress is awesome. It's our first time here. We're just wondering, do you sometimes do special things to get people to come back?"

"Yes, we do. There's a little discount or sometimes dessert. Do you want some dessert?"

"We'll take some dessert."

"I'll bring a piece of cheesecake."

"Well, since there are two of us, can you do any better?"

You might think this is funny and crazy, but if you go out and start practicing, you'll get better at asking. When you buy a car, you negotiate with the salesperson, who rarely can do any negotiating. The sales manager there might make all the decisions on the pricing of the car, but it's the finance manager who makes all the decisions on the financing of the car. Talk with the right decision maker, no matter what the situation. Remember, rarely in life does something work all the time. However, if you try these negotiating tactics many times, they will work some of the time.

price as the beginning step. And the rule of thumb for all negotiating is this: Negotiate only with the decision maker.

Have you ever gone to a restaurant and seen people yelling at the waitress? The food is no good, the chicken is cold, the fish is bad, and the poor waitress is about to cry. She wants to help, but what can she do? Nothing; she's not the decision maker. Then she goes to the manager and the manager comes over to your table. This manager is the person you should complain to . . . the person in charge. Negotiate on a property only with the people who control it and can make a decision. Ask them, "In whose name is the property? Is it yours? Are you the one who can make the ultimate decision to sell?"

Here's a good example of how a few well-selected words can bring in thousands of dollars as a result of skilled negotiations.

When investors call on a house advertised at a price of $200,000, if that's a good deal, they may just offer the listed price. Let's say the property is worth $280,000. The seller tells you it's worth $280,000, and it is. It is a great deal. Many investors would just accept that great deal and have $80,000 of potential profit. Not bad!

However, what if you ask, "Why are you selling?" What if they respond that the mortgage is $150,000 and it's going into foreclosure. The sellers need to pay off the debt—$150,000—plus they need $15,000 cash so they can move. Now you know that they may take $150,000 plus $15,000, or $165,000 instead of $200,000. That one question could possibly save you $35,000.

Then you ask, "Can you do any better? What is the least you would take?" What if they say, "Well, if you could get me $10,000 soon, I'll take it." You just saved or made another $5,000 by asking some key questions. Perhaps you are skeptical and think that this does not work. It definitely does not work if you do not try it! This is exactly what happened to a student of mine, Carl, in Atlanta. By asking those key questions, he made an extra $40,000 on what he knew was already a good deal!

IDENTIFY THE SELLER'S PAIN

In order to find and negotiate good deals where you might be able to get owner's terms, you must find the sellers' pain (i.e., motivation) and deal with it. If they do not have any pain or motivation, then you can't help them and will not get a good deal.

Ask them the following questions:

"Why are you selling?"

"How long do you have to sell?"

"How did you come up with your price?"

If they request all cash, ask them why. What will they do with the cash? Why do they need it?

Be inquisitive like a four-year-old and ask why, why, why. You must discover their true motivation, desires, and fears in order to structure a creative solution that helps them and allows you to get good deals with good terms.

LEAVE YOUR EMOTIONS OUT OF IT

Learn how to walk away from negotiating to get what you want. The less you care, the more money you'll make, because if you're emotionally attached to one property, you won't be a good negotiator.

I learned that lesson when I worked on Wall Street and watched people trading hundreds of millions of dollars of options. It can be painful for traders to lose $5 million of their money or their firm's money or their clients' money. The only way they can do this work is to have no emotion and not care. From what I could see, most behaved like robots; they just analyzed the information and acted, because if they became emotional, their decision-making process became cloudy.

When you're making decisions, don't let emotions get in your way. The one who cares *less* is the one who usually wins. Remember, real estate investing is just numbers. Remove your emotions when you negotiate.

You can negotiate on all aspects of a real estate contract. Of course, you must negotiate on price. Always ask for terms or owner financing, and also negotiate on time to close, closing costs, and all of the aspects of your offers or contracts. These steps will help you make more money and use less of your own money to buy and profit from real estate.

In my standard buyer's contract, the contract I use when I offer to buy a property, the typed-in closing time is 90 days, not 30 days. You will not always get 90 days to close, but if it is in the contract, you may get it sometimes.

CLOSE 90 DAYS OUT

Most contracts in real estate say that closing must occur within 30 days. Try this instead: Set your closings for 90 days out through your standard buyer's contract. (Contracts are covered in the next chapter.)

Let's say you're able to get financing in 20 days or get a partner to come in and buy the property in 30 days or wholesale it to someone in 30 days. If you have 90 days to close on a $200,000 deal, but you can close in 25 days, it's time to renegotiate with the seller. Here's a possible dialogue:

"The closing is 90 days from now. It will be the beginning of April when you get your $200,000. Would you like that money a little sooner?

robert's tip

Follow the example of my Wall Street firm and do a preliminary sale. You'd say, "I think this house is worth $300,000. The repair person told me it needs $10,000 in repairs. A buyer should take $220,000 for it once it's fixed up. If those numbers are correct, that smells like a good deal."

The lesson is to put an offer in *first* with a contingency, *then* do your due diligence. You might come back to the seller and say, "Both you and a repair person thought it would cost $10,000, but repairs are really going to be $50,000. Because it's so messed up, it's not worth $300,000. It's only worth $100,000." Do you get upset? No, you just renegotiate because the deal was misrepresented to you and the numbers weren't right. But if you do your preliminary homework right and the numbers look good, control it first and then study it. Remember, until you have a signed contract, you have nothing. Do not spend all of your time analyzing a property.

In fact, would getting the money in the next three weeks help you?"

The seller says, "Yes, I could pay off my bills and move a little sooner."

A conversation like that gets sellers to visualize and mentally act out what they would do with the money. Then you finally ask this question:

"If I were going to get you cold, hard cash in your pocket sooner, that would help you move sooner and pay off your debt, right?"

Always restate what the other person said and then ask, "Would you take less?" The response might be, "I really don't want to come down. But I tell you what, if you got that money to me quicker, I'd take $199,000."

You made $1,000 just by asking that question. If you're a good negotiator, you could even get the seller down to $195,000 and save another $4,000.

USE TIME WISELY

Remember, you have only one asset in life: time. Please don't waste it agonizing or worrying. Your primary goal is to find a motivated seller, shoot out an offer on the seller's property, and find a way to control that property. That's what you need to focus on like a laser beam so you don't waste time as you travel on your road to riches.

robert's tip

In my first year as an investor, I looked at houses, talked to people, and stood outside the houses waiting for lightning to strike me and tell me to buy a certain property. I was scared to death and I made no offers, bought no real estate, and made no money. That approach is guaranteed to produce zero results for you. I know, I tried it for an entire year.

It's easy to become focused on looking at houses, talking to people, and studying a lot. Those things are all important to do, but it's best to take action that results in making offers. If you never make an offer, you'll never be a real estate investor.

If someone won't talk to you or negotiate on a deal or things aren't going right, your backup plan is to shoot an offer and move on. Maybe the seller says, "I'm not negotiating. I want $400,000. That's it." When that happens, don't take it personally; just keep on moving forward. Make a low offer and then go out and find more motivated sellers.

For most situations, I recommend shooting a low offer in writing and including a contingency clause stating the sale is contingent on the buyer's inspection approval. If the seller signs your low offer, remember, you don't have to buy it; for now, you simply want to *control* that property. Having control gives you the right to inspect the home and make an assessment. Once you've seen the house, it could be so undesirable that you'll want to forget the deal altogether. The contingency clause allows you to get out of an undesirable deal. Caution: Do not put offers in if you do not intend to close on them. However, do your research, put an offer in, and then verify everything. Too many people spend all of their time stricken with paralysis of analysis. Make offers now!

BE A CONFIDENT PLAYER

To become a successful investor who can negotiate good deals and get property without using your own funds, negotiate from a position of power, control, and confidence. Adopt the mind-set that says, "I am finding great deals. I am successful. I have a lot of deals to look at." When doing your real estate business, present yourself as one who is confident, busy, and successful.

That means, as an investor, you don't phone sellers and whine, "Please, I've got to find a deal; sell me a property. What will you take? Can you do any better? Something needs to happen. I need to get one deal, just one. Please help."

I compare this posturing to dating—and no one wants to date a whiner. Imagine if someone came up and said, "I haven't had a date in a couple of years; no one will ever call me back; I don't have any phone numbers; would you please just give me your number and maybe I can call you some day and we can go out."

Not impressive. Instead, people prefer to deal with others who are active. A friend of mine, Doug, is a master at psychology and persuasion. When he was single, he said, "Robert, do you want me to show you how I can get every girl in this place to want to go out with me, dance with me, and ask for my phone number?" I said, "Doug, you know you're not that great-looking—it's not going to happen."

So we went to a bar in which 50 out of 100 people there were women. Doug walked in with a big smile on his face. He's not a good dresser or an overly good-looking guy (sorry, Doug—in fact, people say we look alike). But he approached the most beautiful girl in the bar first and started to chat.

"Hey, how ya doin'? My name's Doug. What's your name?"

"Susan."

"Susan, great to meet you. Hey, I'll be right back. . . ." and he spoke to another woman, saying, "Hey, I'm Doug. What's your name?"

"Judy."

"Judy, I'm Doug. . . ."

"Nice to meet you."

"Judy, do you like to dance?"

"You bet."

"Oh God, that's great. Hey, I'll see ya in a little bit. Okay?"

And he walks over to someone else and asks, "What's your name?"

"Sherri."

"Hey, Sherri, I'm Doug. How are you doing? Are you a student? What are you doing here? Oh great, that's good. Do you like to dance?"

"Sometimes."

"Me, too; not all the time. Hey, I'll be right back. Maybe we can dance later. I gotta go." Each time he talked to one of the women, he was smiling, confident, and enthusiastic.

All of a sudden, every woman (and even the guys) in the bar were talking with Doug and smiling and laughing. Then he went back to each one of the women and asked, "Hey, you want to dance? Great, let's dance." A few minutes later, he said, "I gotta go." Then he would dance with someone else. Before long, all the girls and guys were commenting, "This guy's dancing with all the women and everyone knows him; he's having a great time. I gotta know this guy." Soon they were saying, "Here's my number. Call me." They crowded around him to talk to him. He taught me about posturing.

Can you do what Doug did in your real estate circles? You simply call on some prospective deals and say, "I want to buy 10 properties this month and I'm calling on about 15 houses today. What have you got?" Not a whiner's statement at all. If sellers start pressing you or giving you a hard time, just say, "I gotta go; I've got 20 more houses to look at." Of course, you must always be honest, polite, and sincere, like Doug. If someone offered you 10 houses this month for $10 each, would you buy them? Of course.

In this business, we've got the newspaper to go through and the whole Multiple Listing Service (MLS). Since you can't get to it all, you have to posture and tell prospective sellers what you're doing. Be honest and up front with them. But remember your goal: to write lots of offers, then sign a deal.

NEGOTIATING GUIDELINES

Before we move on to contracts in Chapter 11, let's summarize the essential points from this chapter. First, in terms of communicating:

- Ask kind and understanding questions. Use them to gather information. Probe until you fully understand the seller's situation.

- Listen carefully to the answers, but remember to listen to and trust your inner (gut) feeling, too.

- Use sensitive questioning and listening to identify what the seller really needs and what his or her motivation is. Learn to describe the benefits of your offer in terms of the seller's needs.

- Use your experience and your creativity! There are as many potential solutions as there are needs. Offer no more than is necessary to ful- fill the needs.

Fine-tune your negotiating skills by remembering these valuable rules:

- The one who mentions price or terms first loses.

- Always find out what else the seller can add to the transaction.

robert's tip

If you can't find a deal or you're having trouble getting started, just shoot out five offers a day. If you do that for six months, you can assume *something* is going to happen. But if you don't shoot out any offers and just bite your nails and get stressed out, nothing much will happen. That's guaranteed. Five offers a day keep the blues away.

- Determine whether the seller doesn't need all the cash now—use that knowledge to your advantage!

- Use questions. Avoid declarative sentences.

- When someone answers no, ask, "Why not?"

- Frame your questions to get the answers you want. People are much more motivated to respond with a no than a yes. Make that no mean yes by posing your question like this: "Is there any rea- son why we couldn't consider . . . ?" If no is the answer you get, move on to your proposal.

- Be aware of body language—your own and the seller's. It reveals subconscious thoughts and feelings.

- Never be afraid of silence. Once you have asked a question, *wait* for the answer, no matter how long it takes. Remember, if you are talking, you are not learning. If you must say something, choose your words very carefully.

- Make promises slowly and thoughtfully—they are the foundation of your reputation.

- Never burn your bridges. He or she who becomes angry is out of control and always loses.

- If the deal suits your needs, get a contract (subject to verification of the information) or an option for a period of time long enough to verify every detail.

- If the deal does not suit your needs, always pursue an option. This will give you time to rethink your position and to see if someone else might like to pursue the opportunity.

Negotiating Keys

Key 1.   Stick to questions.

Key 2.   Listen to the answers.

Key 3.   Try to fully understand the situation.

Key 4.   Be friendly, and really listen.

Key 5.   Try to determine what the problem really is.

Key 6.   Do not think about potential solutions until you are certain you and they understand their problem.

Key 7.   *How much* money do they need and how soon do they need it?

Key 8.   Talk about your benefits in terms of their needs.

Key 9.   Keep your financial calculator out of sight.

Key 10.   Keep your emotions out of sight, too.

chapter 11

learning contract basics

It is not for us to forecast the future, but to shape it.
—Antoine de Saint-Exupéry

You found it. You analyzed it. Now you have to control it. Simply put, you have to have a signed offer, a contract. So many investors, beginners or pros, come to me and say, "I've got a great deal worth $1 million, but I can get it for $200,000. I'm going to make $800,000. I'm going to buy it, rent it out, and make so much money every month. It's going to be great!"

Then I ask: "Do you have it under contract? Do you own it?" They say, "No, I'm going to sign the contract next week." They have nothing—and you will have nothing but a lot of excitement until you get a signed contract. Spelling out agreements in legal contracts provides a safety net in real estate transactions.

USE A ONE-PAGE CONTRACT

I recommend using a simple, one-page contract to make your offers. Your offer contract spells out the terms, protects your interests, and includes necessary disclosures and contingencies.

Especially if the seller is motivated and under stress, you don't want to add any confusion by using a complicated, 20-page contract or offer.

Of course, in some states you need a longer contract to buy something, but I still like to keep things simple. If someone is a crook, you could sign a 5,000-page contract and still get ripped off. If someone is honest, you can make a deal happen on just a handshake.

When I worked for a major Wall Street firm, I learned a lot from how companies did their contracts when they'd buy and sell other companies. On one occasion, the firm I worked for was going to buy a $300 million

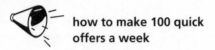

how to make 100 quick offers a week

Once you have a one-page contract set up on your computer, you can create an offer in 30 minutes or less. One of my clients said, "Robert, I don't like to talk to people; I don't like to get out; I'm busy; I'm not a negotiator; I can't do any of this." When I asked if she could make offers, she said, "I have that one-page contract, and you showed us how to complete it with a contingency, so I could probably fill this out on my computer."

She realized it took only a minute or two to type an address and a price on a standard contract, print it, sign it, fold it, and put it in an envelope. So she began sending out 100 offers a week, which cost less than $40 a week (100 letters times the postage). If a house is listed in the Multiple Listing Service (MLS) by a Realtor or advertised in a homes-for-sale magazine or listed in the newspaper for $1 million, she offers close to $500,000 but she uses odd numbers. For example, if a house lists for $1 million, she offers $482,316. If it's listed for $3 million, she offers $1,600,414. If it's listed for $200,000, she offers $99,413.

Every Friday, she tracks her activities: How many offers were sent? How many responses were received? Typically, she gets no response from 95 percent of the offers she sends out. Some respond and write things like, "I can't believe you offered $482,000 for this $1 million home; you're out of your mind! I hate you investors!" About 4 percent give that kind of a response, but the remaining 1 percent accept her offer or call back and say they can't sell for such a low price, but they are motivated. She then negotiates with the motivated sellers, which has led to the purchase of a lot of properties. Of course, she has a contingency clause in all of her contracts so that if the contract is signed she is not obligated to buy the property before she inspects and approves it.

By doing it this way, she gets between four and six deals a month and now owns more than 100 properties bought at 60 to 75 cents on the dollar. If you follow her lead and shoot out a lot of offers, you could make a lot of money, too.

company. To start the ball rolling, representatives from my company simply wrote a letter, which is called *intent to make an offer*. The letter said, "We want to buy your company for $300 million cash, and we'll close in six months contingent upon us doing our due diligence and approving of what we find." It also said this firm would have an exclusive right to buy the company for $300 million, called the *right of first refusal*. This means that up to the time of sale, the company can't entertain any other offers for the duration of the contract.

The prospective buyer certainly controlled that deal when the offer was signed. Only when the decision makers got signatures on that letter did they begin their due diligence. And the contract these big companies signed was one page; I saw it.

STANDARD BUYER'S CONTRACT

Make your contract a form of income for you. If you are buying a property, write at the top of the contract "Standard Buyer's Contract" and follow these directions. (You'll find a sample contract in the appendix.)

Buying Property: Seller Pays Closing Costs

In your buyer's contract, the seller pays for everything, including title insurance and all closing costs. Usually, closing and title insurance costs are split between the buyer and seller, but that does not have to be the case. If it is a rental property, the seller gives the buyer all of the tenants' deposits and the entire month's rent for whenever it is going to close (e.g., if you close on January 15, the contract says you get all of January's rents).

 **make offers via e-mail**

I have a student who sends out 100 offers a week via e-mail. About 90 percent of them go unanswered and 5 percent are answered by recipients (usually Realtors) calling to cuss him out. But 1 or 2 percent make counteroffers, and people often accept ridiculously low prices. Could you do that, too?

I promise you, if you do not include these requirements in your contract, you will never get them. Even if you *do* include them, you will still get them only some of the time. Negotiating these costs can save you hundreds of dollars on every transaction.

Earnest Money

Do you have to put earnest money in a contract? No. The contract is valid without earnest, or up-front, money. However, a lot of Realtors will insist, "I need to make sure you're serious. Put some earnest money down."

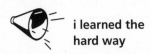

i learned the hard way

Often people sign a contract without really reading it. In the early years of my real estate dealings, someone gave me a standard contract and I went to closing without reading it. Guess who paid for everything? I did. I certainly learned the hard way. I recommend you use your standard contract, and you may not even have to negotiate all of the details.

Again, in most cases, you have a choice—use your own money, or use OPM.

I just put a house valued at $600,000 under contract. The Realtor wanted a lot of earnest money, so I asked him, "How much interest will you pay me on that money?" He said, "I won't pay any interest." So I replied, "I earn about 36 to 40 percent on my money through different real estate investments. That is about 3 percent a month." Would a Realtor be willing to pay that much? Not likely.

Selling Property: Buyer Pays Closing Costs

If you are selling property, you still use your standard contract, but this time, you say the buyer pays the title insurance and closing costs. If it is rental property, the *buyer* gets the deposits but *you collect the rent* for the full month. Type in what you want. You may not get everything you ask for, but if you never ask, you will never get it.

NEGOTIATING OWNER'S TERMS

Now that you have negotiated on price, it is time to negotiate on terms. Whenever you are doing a contract, ask for "owner's terms." Even if you are going to pay cash, even if you are going to wholesale it to someone else, always get owner's terms. That means the *seller* lends you the money to buy the property. You put the least possible amount of money down, so instead of coming up with $100,000 to buy a property, you might put $5,000 down and pay $700 a month.

Most often when you negotiate on owner's terms, the sellers need cash. So you ask this million-dollar question: "What will you do with the

**reminder: only negotiate
with the decision maker**

I know I just told you this in the previous chapter, but it bears repeating
here. Always make sure you are dealing with the person who has the legal
authority to sell the property. If anyone else is involved, make sure you
negotiate with that person, too. You will save a lot of time and hassle when
you communicate directly with decision makers.

Try this: Go to a car dealership, a stereo place, a restaurant, or a major
department store and approach the manager. Ask how much one of the
items costs and say, "What's the least you'll take?" "It's listed for $50, so I
want $50." Respond by saying, "Can you do any better?" Sometimes the
manager will hold firm, but sometimes you might hear this: "Well, we *are*
going to run a sale in three weeks and list it for $29.99, so give me $30
today and it's yours."

If you do not negotiate, you will never get the lower price that you
want. If you negotiate on a real estate deal, you could save thousands of
dollars.

cash?" Here is one answer I have heard: "I need $4,000 to pay off a Visa
bill, and then the rest I'm not sure about." I have learned what that person needs; he just told me about the "pain" he is dealing with. So I say,
"I'll give you $4,000 down so you can pay off your Visa bill, then I'll pay
you $600 a month for the term of the loan." That met his needs and I did
not require much cash as a down payment.

When sellers say, "We're going to invest the cash in a CD and make
5 percent," I ask, "How would you like to earn 7 or 8 percent?" They
reply by saying, "That sounds great. How are you going to do that?" I
respond, "Through owner's terms. Your loan is secured by your real
estate, which you are familiar with, and I will pay you 7½ percent, better
than the bank." By structuring a deal this way through owner's terms, I
help them meet their needs.

CONTINGENCY CLAUSES

On the subject of contracts, let's talk about how to reduce your risk to
zero, because I know you are thinking, "Wait a minute. I'm not sure.
What if I make a bad offer? What if it isn't a good deal? What if it doesn't
rent? What if I am going to lose money?"

Would you be interested in a business if your risk was reduced to zero? The way you do that in real estate is by writing your contract with a *contingency clause*. This clause is also called a *weasel clause*. I rarely sign a contract without one.

In the contract, the contingency clause may say something like this:

- "This contract is contingent upon buyer's inspection and approval before closing . . ."
- "This contract is contingent upon buyer's partner's inspection and approval before closing . . ."
- "This contract is contingent upon buyer receiving favorable financing . . ."

Their messages are all the same: "This is not what I thought it was. It does not work for me. I am out of here." With this clause, you are not obligated to close on a deal if it does not work for you.

Financing Contingencies

Many contracts include a financing contingency: If you do not get proper financing, you do not close on the home. Be careful how often you do this, though. Do not ruin your reputation by putting in offers on properties that you know you cannot close on.

Most people, after signing a contract, choose to close 30 days later. I recommend you type 90 days instead of 30 days into your buyer's contract. Why? Often people who say they will be able to close in 30 days do

a realtor's objection

A Realtor in Miami told one of my students, "Wait a minute. I know you real estate investors like to put in these contingency clauses, but I'm not going to allow it." My student countered, "Listen. What if a hurricane, a flood, a fire, or even vandals come the day before closing, break all of the windows, tear up the property? You mean to say I'd still have to buy it even with these problems? So, just please let me come by the day that we close to check that everything is still okay. I'm a professional real estate investor who's going to close on it if everything seems right, don't worry about that." Yes, it is fair to put in that contingency clause, no matter what a Realtor says.

not do so. In fact, half of all real estate contracts fail because buyers do not get their financing in time.

With a good deal and giving yourself 90 days to close, you can find something to do with that property, like lining up a buyer. You risk not closing, but since you have control of the property, you have reduced *your* risk to zero.

CONTRACT FOR DEED

When you are buying a property, your first preference is always to get the deed to the property. If the seller will not give you the deed (possibly because the mortgage has due-on-sale clauses), then turn to a lease option (discussed in the following section).

Here is an example of a contract for deed, sometimes called a *land contract*. (Another example is included in the appendix.)

Mr. Smith owns the house he bought 10 years ago for $50,000. It is worth $100,000 today. You say, "Mr. Smith, I'll buy it from you for $70,000," and he agrees. But instead of borrowing the money, you give Mr. Smith a contract that says, "I will pay you $700 a month for *x* number of years until I pay all $70,000. I will have the house under contract for deed."

So who owns the house? You do. You get all the benefits of ownership, and, after you fulfill the terms of the contract, you get the deed. This is a type of owner's terms. (Remember, *owner's terms* refers to the seller lending you the money to buy the property.)

CONTROLLING PROPERTIES WITH OPTIONS

Most commercial and industrial property is not controlled with contracts, but with options. An option gives you the *right* to buy something but *not the obligation.* So if you see a $40 million office building and put an option in to buy it at $30 million within one year, the seller will sign and you have one year to buy it for $30 million. Then, whenever you find someone who will pay you $32 million for it, you exercise your option and give the seller $30 million.

Sometimes sellers want a down payment before allowing you to option a piece of property. However, if you are a good negotiator, you will make the down payment as low as possible.

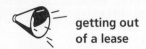

**getting out
of a lease**

Do people get out of leases? Yes. However, I am not recommending you do
a lease option just so you can walk away from it. I recommend doing it
because you have the freedom of not being tied to the property like the
owner would be. You have less liability and risk. And if you have done your
homework and have lease-optioned it properly, you will make money. So it
is possible to get out of a lease, but it is not usually smart.

Remember, a contract with a contingency is almost like an option
because you are not obligated to buy.

Control with a Lease

You can control property through a lease. You also could re-lease it for
more than what you have leased it for (if your lease gives you the right to
sublease). This is another way to make money.

Control with Lease Options

You could lease a property for $500 a month for five years with the option
to buy it. You could also have the right to sublease it for $800 or $1,000
a month or so.

If you lease a property for five years with the option to buy it, you *do
not own* it. What if the world goes into a massive depression? Suppose
you bought the property with borrowed money and then were obligated to
pay it back? You would be in hot water because you would own the property and would have an obligation to pay. With a lease option, even if a
depression hits and the property value goes down by half, you still have
an option to buy but no obligation. (Read Chapter 8 for more in-depth
discussion of lease options.)

PUT IT IN WRITING

As I've said before, my general rule for everything you do is this: Disclose everything in writing.

For example, if I lease-option property from Bill, I have a five-year
lease with a five-year option to buy it, then I turn to Susie and say,

"Susie, would you like to become a homeowner? You can lease-option or buy the property from me. Give me $5,000 down and $1,000 a month." She is now a homeowner who has owner's terms or some kind of ownership in the property. What if Bill (whom I got the property from) suddenly goes bankrupt, gets divorced, or has the IRS chasing him, and he cannot pass clear title? At the same time, Susie says, "I'm ready to exercise my option. I want to buy the property." I would have to say, "I can't sell you the property because I don't have title to it, Bill does, and he is having some financial difficulties." Susie is upset and says, "Hey, I thought you were going to sell me the house." Through these actions, I have committed fraud. That is why you always disclose everything in writing any time you exchange information with someone: a mortgage banker, a title lawyer, a buyer, or a seller. If you do not, you will regret it.

In my standard buyer's contracts, I write this on the top of the cover page:

(1) "I am a real estate investor. I am buying your property and I may resell it or rerent it for a profit. You understand that."

(2) "I do not represent you or your interests."

proper title disclosure

Always make sure there is proper title disclosure for any transaction. Some real estate investors are going to prison for fraud because they did not properly disclose title information. Learn the proper way to do this and you will stay out of trouble. Better yet, have your title company or attorney do the paperwork to ensure it complies with laws in the appropriate city and state. This reflects a decision *not* to become a title expert. You could learn how to do a search, how to file it, and so on, but knowing that won't help you make money. Your job is to buy and sell properties. It's like driving a car. Before you get into it, you don't need to know exactly how everything works. All you need to know is that you stick your key in it, pump in some gas, and go. If the car breaks down, you simply go to a professional who can fix it.

It's the same idea with real estate. Spend your time finding others who are experts in certain areas and hire them. You just need to use your key, turn it on, and go.

Have I disclosed everything I am doing?

When I am going to sell a property (using a standard seller's contract) or lease-option it, I also state in writing:

(1) "I am a real estate investor who invests in real estate to make money."

(2) "I do not represent you or your interests."

(3) "I may or may not have or be able to obtain good title to this property."

Most people say I am being overly cautious, but as you know by now, I strongly believe in disclosing everything in writing.

CONTRACT REVIEW

1. Negotiate a contract. Negotiate, negotiate, negotiate. You can always get a lower price. If the seller quickly accepts your price, you have not negotiated enough.

2. Always try to get owner's terms.

3. Always include contingency clauses to reduce your risk.

If you cannot do these things, then you have to make a business decision based on all your information and decide if it is worth it for you to proceed or walk away. Rule of thumb: *Always have more pending deals than you can do.*

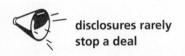 **disclosures rarely stop a deal**

You might say, "Wait a minute. If you put these disclosures in your contracts, no one will sign them." Not in the real world! Most people are motivated for their own reasons. If a buyer wants to become a homeowner, he or she is willing to overlook that clause. Motivated sellers want their money. You have found their pain. They are willing to go ahead. But if you do not disclose everything and something bad happens, you could be in big trouble. It's called fraud.

Also, be sure to understand how to control properties by contracts, contract for deed, and putting in contingency clauses, options, and lease options. Make sure you disclose everything. Never, *ever* close on a property without getting the proper title insurance and having the proper insurance in place to protect you.

learning how to find funding sources and manage your credit

Money is always there but the pockets change; it is not in the same pockets after a change, and that is all there is to say about money.
—Gertrude Stein

Most people who invest in real estate make money in only one or two ways: They buy properties and borrow money from the bank to do so, or they deal in mortgages. But many more sources for funding and profiting from your real estate investments exist. You can use these sources of funds to buy property. Do not use your own money. Create money from other sources to get into real estate.

MORTGAGE ORIGINATION

If you're actively buying or selling property, you're *initiating*, *referring*, or *acquiring* mortgages. It's customary to be paid for these services by affiliating with a mortgage company, a mortgage broker, or network marketing companies that do mortgages.

Affiliate with some good mortgage brokers or become one yourself. Go to a variety of mortgage companies—at least one main company plus two or three secondary ones—and research the best deals available at a given point in time.

Investors (and others) who attract customers needing a mortgage are called *mortgage originators*. Originators are paid anywhere from 30 to 70 percent of the up-front fees on a mortgage—just for marketing and bringing in customers. For example, if a mortgage broker is working on a $200,000 mortgage that has two points ($4,000), the originator would receive half, or one point ($2,000), for filling out the application and helping to start the loan process. I suggest you should get about half, or at least 20 to 25 percent, of the points for referring mortgages to a mortgage company. A lot of times, you can actually become an employee of the mortgage company, so you don't have to be licensed. (Since every state is different, check with a local mortgage company about these requirements. Also note that in some states, paying fees to mortgage originators is illegal.) Please send me an e-mail if you want to learn about affiliating with a mortgage company. My email is: robertshemin@the-beach.net.

REFERRAL FEES

You can also negotiate for marketing, referral, or consulting fees as you develop marketing relationships with mortgage companies and brokers. Make arrangements to receive something in exchange for bringing in customers—either money or goods (a desk, computers, etc.). Make this a worthwhile way to legally and ethically bring in rewards for your valuable referrals.

For the first five years I was in real estate, I often referred people to service providers I knew and trusted. In fact, I'd refer 40 to 60 mortgages a year to the best mortgage company I could find. When I decided I wanted remuneration for these referrals, I went to the decision makers at this mortgage company, who agreed to pay me 50 percent of the referral fees. The company keeps the other 50 percent for its efforts. This is a fairly standard commission. The originator, the person who brought in the business, gets about half of the profit or points.

You can apply this concept to related services, too. For example, you

---

think about it

Whether you are a beginner or a pro, how many deals might you be involved in doing during the next . . .

One year? _____

Five years? _____

Ten years? _____

Twenty years? _____

If you could get referral fees for mortgages, closing and title services, repair and contractor services, property insurance, consulting, and/or any other services your buyers and sellers might need, how much could you make?

_____

Let's say you are involved in 20 properties and/or sales in the next year. If you got a mortgage referral fee of only $500 per loan, that would be an extra $10,000 to you. Do the math.

---

can develop referral relationships with insurance agents for your contacts who need renters' or homeowners' insurance. You can also refer them to contractors or people who do repairs in exchange for a fee of 10 to 20 percent. By doing so, you provide a service that brings business to them that they wouldn't otherwise have had. You deserve compensation for that service.

However, be sure to handle your referral fees correctly. First, put every detail of your agreement in writing so it's clearly understood by everyone involved. Specifically spell out the amount of your fee and exactly when and how it will be paid. Second, make sure you have no liability in the arrangement you set up. For example, if you refer a certain contractor, make it clear that you don't *guarantee* his or her work. In fact, encourage your contacts to do their own research beyond your referral.

Referrals on title work can be another source of fees. Some large real estate companies get referral fees from title companies for sending them customers—approximately 20 percent of the title closing fees. For this example, assume the title insurance premium on a $500,000 house was between $1,500 and $3,000, with 70 to 90 percent of that being profit to the title company. It charges closing fees of $200 to $500 and document preparation fees of $50 to $200. Therefore your referral fee could be 20 percent of the title, premium, and some or all of the closing costs.

I suggest you find a good title company and negotiate referral fees with the decision makers. After all, other real estate investors are making good money doing so.

BANKING RELATIONSHIPS

A great source for buying property is through banks. If you have some good deals, a good business plan, and some good credit, getting funds from a bank may enable you to buy property without putting any of your own money into the deal.

Here's how I bought over 100 properties without using my own money: I went to a bank and got a $100,000 line of credit secured by my own house. The bank also agreed to do 15-year loans on any property I owned at a 75 percent loan to value. That is, if a house had a value of $100,000, the bank would lend $75,000 (75 percent).

For example, I would find a deal that was worth $100,000 from a motivated seller who would sign an offer to sell it to me for $70,000. I would use the bank's money (the line of credit) to pay the seller $70,000 cash. One month later, when the house looked better and I had rented or lease-optioned it, I would ask the bank for a permanent 15-year loan. The house would be appraised for at least $100,000. The bank would lend me $75,000 (75 percent), which I would use to pay off the loan or put back into my line of credit. Then my line of credit would again be $100,000 to pay cash for another house. Not one cent of my own money would be used. Caution: *Never borrow money you are not positive that you can pay back.* Also, be careful about borrowing against your own home; if the loan is not paid back on time, you could lose your home.

If you do not have great credit or the ability to do this, find someone who does have that ability. (We talk about how to restore your credit later in the chapter.) Whatever you lack in business, find someone who can help you. You probably know or can find people who want to make money in real estate and have great credit, but who don't have the time, energy, or knowledge to make it happen. You can develop the knowledge and use your energy to find the deals. Let others borrow the money. You can partner with them 50-50, 60-40, 70-30, or whatever works for both of you.

Always make sure you have a good deal lined up before you borrow any money. Have a built-in cushion, too, as well as an exit strategy. If someone else is borrowing the money for your deals, make *triple* sure it's a good deal.

Also begin establishing good relationships with a bank. When I started out, I went to the bank almost every month to ask for a loan. Every month the answer was no. Then, the fifteenth time, the answer was maybe, and soon after it was yes. The bank gave me a $50,000 loan on a duplex worth $80,000.

robert's tip

I challenge you, regardless of the status of your money or credit, to fill out a financial application, go to a bank or mortgage company, and get preapproved to buy something. It's a good exercise to see where you stand. I'm not saying go out and borrow money; I'm saying start building that relationship. Then you'll find out what you need to do to improve your credit and be able to borrow funds.

At that time, I had more money on deposit in the bank than I was able to borrow. But the way banks work, after you borrow once, you can borrow again—and then again. You may find that when you borrow only $100,000, the bank doesn't really care about you. But when you borrow over $1 million, the bank cares! Loan officers start calling—how are you feeling, how's business, let's go to dinner, and so on.

HARD MONEYLENDERS

You'll find hard moneylenders in every major town. These people have a lot of money (or access to it), and they may lend it to you—at high interest rates—on the deals you want to buy. They don't care much about your credit. For instance, if the mortgage rate today is 6 to 8 percent, some hard moneylenders may charge 10 to 15 percent. And instead of charging 1 or 2 points (i.e., 1 or 2 percent of the loan amount) as a bank or mortgage company would, they charge between 2 and 10 points. If you want to borrow $100,000, a hard moneylender might charge a $10,000 fee plus 15 percent interest to borrow money for that home. Obviously, if you already have the cash or have good enough credit to satisfy the bank, borrow the money you need elsewhere. Going to a moneylender is a last resort.

The biggest advantage of getting funding through hard moneylenders

robert's tip

Don't be greedy. If you stand to make $30,000 on a deal and can get it done quickly and easily by paying a hard moneylender $5,000 in points and interest, so be it. A lot of investors say, "I'm not going to pay that much interest. That's too much." But, moving forward, the important question to ask is "How much will I make on this deal?"

Never let cost get in the way of profit. If it's profitable, do it.

is that they really don't care about your credit. Plus they can respond quickly, while banks and mortgage companies are still collecting four wheelbarrows full of paper and taking 30 or 90 days to process your loan.

You always want a source of hard money in case a bank won't fund your promising and profitable deals. So your homework is to look in the newspaper for ads that say "We Lend Money," then meet with two or three of these lenders and develop good relationships in case you want to borrow from them in the future. Also, go to your local real estate investors association meeting to meet other investors and lenders. (And check out www.robertshemin.com.)

PROGRAMS FOR EVERYONE

I suggest you learn every possible way to finance mortgages and use them so you are never stuck *not* being able to do a deal because you don't have access to funds.

Normally, when you buy a house, you get a new mortgage to buy it. If the house costs $1 million, you borrow $900,000 and put $100,000 down. Depending on your credit, income, and the collateral or property, the bank or mortgage company will determine how much it will lend you. A homeowner's loan, meaning you are going to live in the property, is less risky for a lender than a loan for a non-owner-occupied property or an investor loan. People are less likely to default on a home loan and risk losing their residence. Of course, there are hundreds or thousands of loan programs out there, and you'll find one that's right for you.

GIVE YOURSELF GOOD CREDIT

Good credit is vital to your success as a real estate investor. Simply put, your credit is important because it affects what you pay for money, whether for your cars, your life insurance, and for sure any properties you buy. Specifically, when you're buying a property, it affects your ability to borrow. When you're selling property, your buyers' credit affects you. Half of all real estate contracts fail because the people can't qualify for financing, and knowing about credit restoration will help not only you, but also your buyers. And the most important thing you need to know is that the only people who can legally and ethically help restore your credit, if need be, are yourself, a credit counseling service, your attorney, or a licensed financial planner.

I've had so many buyers who think they are unable to buy a home because their credit is awful and they have no down payment. Then, 60 days later, they're buying a home because we helped them qualify for the down payment. We have also helped them increase their credit or use some creative financing techniques to take possession of the property. Let's go over some of these. This will help you buy and sell.

About half of all credit reports have a mistake in them, so you need to get a copy of *all* your credit reports. People can call credit companies and request copies of their credit reports. They're also available at www.shemin.com. Get a copy of yours and look it over. If there are mistakes, you need to write in and have those taken off. You can do that yourself, or you can hire an attorney or someone to represent you.

Challenge whatever bad information is in the report, and keep challenging it until it's removed. Under federal law, the credit reporting agencies have 30 days to respond, and sometimes they don't have the workers or the time to research and verify the information. If they can't do that within 30 days, they have to remove the offending words.

Understand that the law also says these companies don't have to react to frivolous claims, so there's a little leeway for them, but what often happens is that credit repair companies just keep challenging the facts (e.g., the date is wrong, the amount is wrong, this isn't mine). Simply for lack of people power, a bad rating may be softened. That's what so-called credit repair companies do—they keep challenging and challenging and challenging.

If an incorrect report isn't fixed, you have the right to request the original loan documents. A lot of people don't know that, and sometimes they can't produce them. That might also remove the credit problem. Certain bankruptcies are not reported accurately, and sometimes the bankruptcy courts don't respond when the credit repair companies call them to verify. Some people have told me that even bankruptcies may be removed just by challenging them. Again, credit rating companies don't have the time to respond. However, the challenges can't be frivolous. But who decides what's frivolous? A lot of people find that just by challenging a report in writing, items are taken off.

You can do this yourself or you can get a professional to help you. Lots of credit repair companies say they can do it. Some of my buyers have tested one service that's actually run by attorneys. It's called www.CreditLawyer.com. I am not affiliated with them, but I've seen people get real results because they work with real attorneys. They're on the Internet, they charge $50 a month, and they usually work with people for three to five months. (Also see Chapter 13, under "Legal Protection." It discusses a company called Pre-Paid Legal Services, Inc., which provides its members with attorneys who have achieved good results for some people because they know how to write effective letters.)

Get a copy of your credit report, check it, and challenge anything that's incorrect. Challenge anything you don't think should be on there and keep challenging. Make sure you do it with all three of the major credit bureaus, Equifax, Experian, and Trans Union.

Do things that improve your credit, and don't do things that hurt it. Be very careful about who checks your credit. When you lease or buy a car, sometimes the dealership sends out requests to eight or nine finance companies and checks your credit eight or nine times. All that activity knocks down your credit score. Ask everyone how they check your credit and how it will affect your credit score.

If you have a special situation that affects your ability to pay your bills (e.g., divorce or illness), you can write a nonemotional explanation, up to 100 words, and attach it to your credit report. Bottom line? Understand credit so you can help your potential buyers.

Once you have found a reliable source (or sources) of funding and have ensured that your credit rating is tip-top, you'll need to learn how to protect your properties and your newfound wealth. That's the topic of Chapter 13.

learning to protect yourself, your properties, and your wealth

If a man has money, it is usually a sign, too,
that he knows how to take care of it.

—Edgar Watson Howe

Many real estate beginners are scared to start investing because of the risk. With proper knowledge, correct disclosures and business practices, and an understanding of basic asset protection, you can and will be protected. Let's start by discussing the issue of solvency.

FINANCIAL SOLVENCY

If you are sued and you've put assets in corporations, a lawyer could charge you with fraudulent conveyance. How do you defend against it? Show that you were solvent at the time of asset transfer when you made these corporations and trusts. Fill out a financial statement this week and sign and date it. You want it to show that you're solvent, that your assets are greater than your liabilities. If you don't do that and you are sued a year from now, it might be hard to prove. Put everything in writing and file it carefully.

Some of you have tried this asset protection program: No assets equals no worries. But let's say you don't have any money and your insurance is inadequate and you're being sued. How would the lawyers collect the $800,000 (or millions of dollars) they think they deserve? They would wait until you got a job. Judgments are good for anywhere from 7 to 10 years in many states. Good lawyers might wait 10, 20, or even 30 years, hoping that you go to college, get a job, and make money. Then, whenever you have some money or a bank account or a house you want to purchase, they attach your assets. It's called *garnishment*, and it's similar to child support and alimony.

If you have money, who might come after you? Plaintiffs, lawyers, the government, the IRS, the EPA, the ex-spouse, upset business partners, or even clients. Start thinking about asset protection now even if you don't have any assets, because things can happen later. The following are ways you can start to protect your assets.

Avoid Risky Activities

You may think that sounds crazy, because it's just common sense. However, one of the most risky activities in real estate is property management. Managing tenants is the most sued profession in the world, even more so than being a doctor. You may want to stop landlording, which is what I did by setting up my friend in a management company. He wanted to become a property manager, so I helped him form a company, which he's proud to own. He follows my policy and procedures, but if the tenants are going to sue someone, they'd sue him, because he's the manager. He carries a lot of liability. Perhaps you, too, can hire a property management firm and pass on your liability.

Work with, Not against, People

Who sues other people? Angry people. The lady who spilled hot McDonald's coffee and burned herself went to the managers and said, "I have a dry-cleaning bill and I may have some medical bills. Will you do

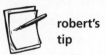

robert's tip

Look at the activities you're doing and see if you can pass them on to somebody else. For one thing, stop driving. That's a risky activity. I'm not a very good driver; I find it stressful and a waste of time, so I live in places where I don't have to drive. I walk, take cabs, and hire a driver.

I found an ad for someone who wanted to own his own limousine company, so I helped Limo John set up a limo company. He drives me around during the week as I go about my business. I sit in the back, talk on the phone, relax, and work. If I can make 10 more phone calls in a day and find one more deal, I've paid for the limo. He drives me around during the week, and on weekends he picks up bachelor parties, weddings, and promgoers and charges $60 an hour. We split the money, so the limo company pays me. I make money and at the same time eliminate a risky activity.

anything?" The McDonald's managers said no way, we don't want to hear about it. She became angry, then pursued her complaint on up the chain of command and got the same reaction. They didn't take care of it. She became angrier. It would have been a good policy to say, "Let's not make our customers angry." They could have paid her cleaning bill and offered her a couple of free Big Macs. She might not have been as angry. Instead, McDonald's chose to save some money and ended up with a multi-million-dollar lawsuit.

Most landlords, landladies, and real estate investors will try to save $200 by not fixing a commode or $50 by not meeting a tenant halfway—and then end up with a $500,000 lawsuit.

Stop doing things that could make people angry; always work with them; be on their side. It's not worth it to make people angry and risk being sued. Weigh the real costs and benefits. Set policies and procedures and follow them.

Don't Have Employees

If you have employees, you're responsible for everything they do and everybody they run over. That's high liability. You can perhaps eliminate the risk of having employees by making them subcontractors. Tell them to do whatever job they're doing, setting their own hours, following the subcontractor agreements, and becoming self-employed. I once had 18 employees who helped me manage my properties, did repairs, and so on. One day I made them all subcontractors. It was one of the best days of my life—reducing the headache and liability of having to manage employees.

Don't Do Repairs Yourself

If you repair something and it breaks and someone gets hurt, you'll probably be held responsible. One of my best friends in Nashville bought a house to fix up and sell. His contractor was repairing the deck, and my friend went out and helped him. He sawed wood, carried supplies, and helped nail part of the deck together. They built the deck, sold the house, and did a good job. The deck could safely hold 18 people. When the people who bought the house had a party, there were 30 people on the deck and it fell; 12 of them went to the hospital in an ambulance. They sued the contractor and won more than $1 million.

They also sued the owner. He called his insurance company, but his liability insurance didn't cover him for construction. He had been acting as a contractor without a contractor's or builder's insurance. Fortunately, he had implemented some of the asset protection tools you're about to learn. If he hadn't, they could have attached everything he owns personally, including his bank account. However, he had set things up properly in limited liability companies and some real trusts, and he negotiated a $3,000 settlement. Stop being a contractor; stop doing your own repairs. Pass that high-liability business on to the general contractor. Remember, you are responsible and may not be insured for all the activities you are tempted to engage in.

Don't Own Things Yourself

That would protect you from being sued. One of my best friends owns more than 20,000 units of real estate and is worth a lot of money. Beyond that, he owns nothing. He drives a 1989 Honda Prelude owned by his company. LLCs and trusts own everything else. If you sue him, you probably won't get anything.

TOOLS FOR ASSET PROTECTION

Let's discuss a variety of ways you can protect your assets.

Form Your Support Team

Start assembling your team now so they're in place as you expand your real estate investing business. Get mortgage brokers and bankers on your team and tell them your plan (e.g., to do 1 deal a month or 1 deal a year or 20 deals a year; to buy and rehab 30 houses a year; to wholesale one property a month). Once you've made your plan, show it to them and say, "I'd like to work with you, and we can both profit. I'll send you business and we can work together."

In addition to a mortgage broker, you'll need a real estate agent, an appraiser, a property manager, other successful investors, and two or three good referred contractors (because you'll need to do repairs on your properties). (You'll also need good legal protection, and this is so important I discuss lawyers in a separate section later in the chapter.)

To find good people for your support team, go to meetings of your local real estate association or your local apartment association and ask people these questions:

- "Who's a good mortgage broker? Who do you use?"
- "Who's a good property manager?"
- "Who is a good mortgage broker and gets the deals done?"
- "Who's a good real estate attorney?"
- "Which closing company or title company do you recommend?"
- "Which contractors do you recommend?"

Go to my web site, www.robertshemin.com, to get a list of real estate associations and referrals for good loans and attorneys.

Once you've gathered names and phone numbers of people referred to you, sit down and talk with these referrals. Maybe even take them to lunch. They'll help you do business and answer your questions, too. Make arrangements to either pay them for their time or refer business to them in exchange for their help. When your sister wants to buy a house, speak up and say, "I know a good mortgage broker. I know a good title person." You may even get part of the commission for the referral. Because they're making money from your contacts, they'll be happy to help your business and answer your questions.

You'll quickly see how developing good relationships with these key

Identifying Your Team Worksheet

Find three good Realtors who can help you find good deals, run comparable sales, and sell some of your good deals. List them here:

_____ _____ _____

Find three good real estate attorneys and a title company that can help you with contracts, closings, and business referrals. List them here:

_____ _____ _____

Find three great mortgage brokers to help you and your clients fund purchases. List them here:

_____ _____ _____

Identify a great real estate accountant who deals with real estate investing. List that person here:

_____

Locate five money partners to help you fund your deals. List them here:

_____ _____ _____

_____ _____

Select two hard moneylenders who make loans on properties (do some networking at local real estate meetings or look in the newspaper). List them here:

_____ _____

Find seven serious real estate investors who are actively buying properties. You can find them at your real estate meeting, in the newspaper, or at auctions. You can wholesale properties to them. List them here:

_____ _____ _____

_____ _____ _____

_____

Choose three good, referred, licensed contractors or handy people who can help you and your clients repair properties and do repair bids. List them here:

_____   _____   _____

Find two older, perhaps retired, successful businesspeople to consult with you on your general business plans, policies, and procedures. Some cities have a SCORE group. (SCORE is an acronym for Service Corp of Retired Executives, a nonprofit organization with chapters across the country.) Call a large bank or the Small Business Administration for a referral to a local SCORE group, retired executives, and businesspeople who can help you for a small fee or for free. List them here:

_____   _____

Take a few successful real estate investors to lunch once a week. Ask them how they find deals, how they fund them, and what you can do to help them.

Lunch partners:

Week 1 _____

Week 2 _____

Week 3 _____

Week 4 _____

Week 5 _____

Week 6 _____

Week 7 _____

Week 8 _____

people fuels your business because they know potential sellers, motivated sellers, property managers, mortgage bankers, Realtors, and potential buyers. Make them part of your inner circle, your board of directors, your team, your advisory counsel.

In fact, set up a plan. Every week, interview people and add one more really good member to your real estate investment team. As you do, you'll learn a tremendous amount. You'll find deals and buyers and money. And your belief in yourself will go up with every referral they send your way!

In order to be a successful real estate investor and buy property without using your own money, you must have a team. Use this Identifying Your Team Worksheet to help you put yours in place.

Get Adequate Insurance Coverage

I had a terrible car accident when I was a teenager. If my parents hadn't had any insurance on the car when I had this horrible wreck, they would have lost everything they owned: the house, the car, the bank account, the savings account. These assets would probably have been attached by the courts to pay for the judgment on the accident. Fortunately, my father had just paid an extra $140 a year for a $1 million umbrella policy, which protected us from losing everything.

I suggest you pull out your car insurance policies, real estate policies, and land policies, and read the exceptions. Property insurance usually doesn't cover nuclear war, terrorism, and mismanagement of city water. If the city floods and water ruins your house, your insurance probably doesn't cover it. Know your exceptions. For example, insurance doesn't cover you for any criminal charges. If you fall asleep at the wheel of your car and cause a wreck (or your teenager does) and somebody dies, you may be charged with manslaughter, and your car insurance would not pay for criminal defense. This is a big hole in your asset protection plan.

If you have mutual funds and bank accounts in your name, you could lose them in a lawsuit, too, so what I do is wrap my investments in an insurance contract, in a life insurance variable annuity based on mutual funds. If I'm sued, they can't get to these assets, because it's almost impossible to attach any type of life insurance contract. To safeguard your money, you may want to sock it away in life insurance.

Set Up a Trust and an LLC

To take your home out of the public domain, transfer it into a land trust or an irrevocable trust. I don't understand why people who set up living trusts or irrevocable trusts use their own names (e.g., the Anderson Family Living Trust). If you're doing it for anonymity, why use your name? All of my trusts are titled after the property address (e.g., the 1010 Jones Street Trust for the house on 1010 Jones Street). If someone does a title search and looks up "Robert Shemin," that house doesn't show up. Transferring your house into a land trust gives you anonymity and some protection.

When you start making money, set up a limited liability company for each bucket of activities. If you own some rental properties, put those in an LLC. Maybe you're doing a lot of wholesaling—have a separate LLC that does that, and you can still write off everything. Most attorneys and accountants recommend setting up an LLC if you own real estate.

LEGAL PROTECTION

Once you begin to develop various sources of real estate income, you will also start to worry about protecting them, so you want to work with good lawyers. I recommend Pre-Paid Legal Services, Inc., which I have used almost weekly for the last several years. You can find an attorney on your own who may or may not be good and who will charge you anywhere from $150 to $300 an hour. However, Pre-Paid Legal Services, Inc., will help save you a lot of money on attorney's fees and also give you the ability to contact top attorneys in any area of the law you need.

I am an independent associate with Pre-Paid Legal Services. I became involved with this company a few years ago and now market its services. Pre-Paid Legal Services is a New York Stock Exchange company. Available all over the United States and Canada, Pre-Paid Legal Services has been in business for more than 30 years (so the organization must be doing something right). Many different people—magazine

for clarification

The information included here about Pre-Paid Legal Services, Inc., is a general overview. Please remember that only the plan contract and associate agreement can give actual terms, coverage, amounts, conditions, and exclusions.

columnists, professionals, experts—are recommending this organiza-tion. *Forbes, Fortune,* the *Wall Street Journal, HR, Human Resource,* and almost every major business and insurance publication have, in the past few years, reported favorably on Pre-Paid Legal Services, Inc. As a mat-ter of fact, the American Bar Association has published a quote that says, "Americans have come to view legal assistance as a necessity. The best way for the majority of Americans to be able to assure themselves of legal assistance when they need it is through a prepaid legal plan." Notice the quote says "the best way." That is a powerful statement.

Basically, every legal need you have ever had, do have, or will have is covered under featured aspects of the Pre-Paid Legal plan. There are five areas of coverage, plus some bonuses. (The following reflects my views about Pre-Paid Legal Services, Inc., and not necessarily those of the company.)

Get Preventive Legal Insurance

For a small monthly fee—generally $26—you, your spouse, and your children (through college age) are covered for legal fees in the United States and parts of Canada.

Especially if you are a real estate investor, you will want to ask lawyers a lot of questions. "What do I do if my tenants do _____? What is the lease-option rule? What should I do when I am having trouble with my contractor? How do I collect money owed to me? What do I do when the bank does not treat me fairly? Is the information the mortgage company told me accurate?" Any time you have legal ques-tions, you can call your Pre-Paid Legal attorney and get answers. Whatever is on your mind—a simple $50 problem or a complicated $500,000 problem—pick up your phone. You get almost unlimited telephone consultation for personal or business questions. Yes, both personal and business.

If you do not have a prepaid legal plan and call an attorney, an hour-long consultation will likely cost you between $100 and $300. With Pre-Paid Legal Services, Inc., if you call and ask questions, your legal bill is simply $26 a month.

If your attorney deems it necessary or appropriate, he or she will write a letter or make a phone call on your behalf. If your car does not get fixed properly, for example, and you call your Pre-Paid Legal law firm, your

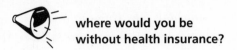

**where would you be
without health insurance?**

You may be asking, "What kind of attorneys do I get for $26?" After all, it is an insurance-type program, a pooled program. So I ask this question: If you have health insurance, how do you expect to afford a good surgeon for $200 a month? It is the same with legal services.

lawyer there would write the repair shop on the firm's stationery demanding the shop make the situation right. "Fix this car . . . pay her the money . . . finish the paint job" or whatever the issue. Most law firms would charge a lot of money for that, but Pre-Paid Legal Services, Inc., covers it.

Sometimes people say, "Robert, I don't like attorneys very much. I don't use them. I don't want to use them. I don't need this service, even though I heard it is a great company and they have great attorneys." Then I ask this: "Have you in the last year or two, or will you in the next year or two, sign any contracts or documents? Will your family sign any contracts or documents?" Buying a car, borrowing money, buying a house, employment agreements, lease agreements, health club agreements, cell phone agreements? Who wrote all those contracts and documents you sign? Attorneys. *Their* attorneys, not yours. So you actually are involved with attorneys all the time, but they do not represent your interests.

People in wealthy families say, "Let me run it past my law firm,"

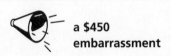

**a $450
embarrassment**

When I was buying a used car, I looked at the contract (I am an attorney, you see) and said, "It looks fine to me." But I decided to fax it to my Pre-Paid Legal Services, Inc., law firm because this service was already paid for. A lawyer looked at the contract and said, "Robert, this is a used car. They're charging you a $450 destination charge. There is no destination if you buy a used car." I felt embarrassed but was glad he saved me $450.

How many contracts are you going to sign in which you will fail to catch something important? Let experts at your law firm review them, too.

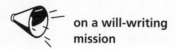

on a will-writing mission

I confess that I am involved in Pre-Paid Legal Services, Inc., because I have a mission . . . to get everyone to put together a will.

I often speak in front of groups and present Pre-Paid Legal as an employee benefit to a lot of small, medium, and large companies. A while ago, I presented to a group in Nashville, Tennessee, and one of my friends from high school attended the meeting. Of about 30 employees there, most of them signed up for Pre-Paid Legal that day because they saw its value and wanted to get their wills done.

However, my friend did not sign up, so I asked him, "You're married and have two children. Why don't you get your will done?" He replied, "I'm going to think about it." I said, "What's to think about? It's $26 a month with a one-time $10 sign-up fee. Get your will done. If you don't want to continue the service, you are not locked in. Just get your will done."

Six weeks later, while he and his wife were still thinking about it, they were driving around town. They had stopped at a red light and a drunk driver ran the light, rammed into their car, and killed them both. The two sets of grandparents cared deeply about the children, but unfortunately, the children had to go into the custody of the state because the parents had no will to express their wishes.

before they sign anything. After you sign up for Pre-Paid Legal Services, Inc., you can send your contracts (up to 10 pages, unlimited personal issues and a few business issues a year) to a law firm in the program and have a lawyer review your paperwork.

Write a Comprehensive Will

The first thing Pre-Paid Legal Services, Inc., does for its members is handle writing a comprehensive will. (If you do not have a will, you are not alone. Eighty percent of Americans do not have wills either.) A top estate-planning attorney charges $500 to $1,000 to write up a will, and charges even more for people with complex estates. The company immediately takes care of the will of the member as part of the $26 per month fee.

If you want strangers to decide where your children and your possessions go at your death, then do not get a will. If you care, then you absolutely need one.

I had some associates who never thought disaster would strike, but they perished when the World Trade Center collapsed in September 2001. I had told them many times, "Get your will done. Sign up for Pre-Paid Legal Services, Inc.," and they did not do it. Their estates are now in big trouble because they did not have the basic document that would have protected their assets—a will. Everyone needs to have one. Get your will done, please! Pre-Paid Legal Services, Inc., will make your will for you and even review it once a year.

Gain Representation in Court

Once you have been a member of Pre-Paid Legal Services, Inc., for 14 days, if you get a speeding ticket (or your teenager does) anywhere in the United States, the company will send a lawyer to court for you in most cases. Now, these lawyers cannot get your tickets thrown out for you, but they can go to court for you and plead to get your points reduced. The bonus is that you do not have to miss work while the lawyers work for you.

Do you have a big hole in your insurance program? Find out today. If you are criminally charged (like with manslaughter or vehicular homicide), your car insurance will not pay for your defense but Pre-Paid Legal will. Assuming you were not high on drugs or alcohol when the accident happened, this service will provide unlimited defense—win, lose, or draw. If you are not worried about being named in a civil lawsuit, you should be. It could happen and, if you are not a Pre-Paid Legal Services member, you will have to find an attorney, pay a retainer fee, and defend yourself—whether you have done anything wrong or not. When you sign up for Pre-Paid Legal Services, Inc., you automatically have 75 hours of top attorney time a year to defend or consult with you. Go to www.prepaidlegal.com for full details.

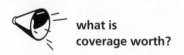
what is
coverage worth?

What is 75 hours of top attorney time worth? It may not get you a trial as big as O. J. Simpson's, but it will get you a good start. It might be worth $15,000, $20,000, or $30,000 of attorney time in the bank. Every year you remain a member of Pre-Paid Legal Services, that benefit increases. After five years as a member, I have 335 hours of top lawyer time (even though I have been named in some little civil lawsuits because I do a lot of business).

OTHER BENEFITS

Prepaid Legal and Tax Advice

When it comes to taxes, as a Pre-Paid Legal Services, Inc., member, you will receive 50 hours of tax attorney time if you are named in an IRS audit on your personal tax return. You can also call your tax attorney and ask tax-related legal questions as you prepare your taxes.

If you are dealing with a legal issue outside of the regular covered services, Pre-Paid Legal will give you a discounted price when you do need to pay a lawyer's fees. In my state, instead of $200 or $300 an hour, Pre-Paid Legal Services, Inc., has negotiated a discount to $95 an hour. Other firms may charge you 50 percent of their normal fee.

Access to Top Law Firms

Of your $26 a month, a good portion pays for lawyers. Pre-Paid Legal puts out millions of dollars each month to top law firms whose lawyers are happy to answer your questions and do your wills. This system *attracts* excellent law firms. All firms in the network are rated A, B, C, or D. An A rating means the firm performs in the top 5 or 8 percent of all law firms. In most states, Pre-Paid Legal Services, Inc., uses only A-rated attorneys and their firms. That means they are the biggest and best, and they offer full service.

Can they do real estate law? Can they do divorce law? Bankruptcy law? Criminal law? Tax law? Insurance law? Yes, they are the biggest, best law firms around the country, and you can have access to them.

Legal Access 24/7

Included in that $26 per month is 24-hour-a-day, seven-day-a-week access to attorneys. (It's available in most states. Services do vary from state to state, so read Pre-Paid Legal brochures and contracts carefully.) If you were ever pulled over, detained, questioned, or arrested by the police, you could reach a lawyer to get help.

The police have a tough job. Most of them are great people, but if they pull my car over in the middle of the night, I am scared because I do not always know my rights. Do I have to answer their questions? Can they look in my trunk? Do I have to tell them if I was doing something wrong?

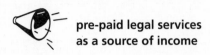

pre-paid legal services as a source of income

I got started in Pre-Paid Legal Services while making real estate deals, talking to other investors, and getting to know landlords and property managers. As we talked, I would say, "By the way, I found this really great service." I would pull out a brochure and an application (even though I was not selling the service at the time). I just saw it as valuable. Then I found out I could actually turn these recommendations into a business as an independent associate.

Pre-Paid Legal Services can even be another income source for you. Becoming a sales representative requires going through training and sticking with it so you can make it work for you. If you are interested, we will work with you using our resources and Internet training as well as training and meetings in most major cities. In addition to hosting conference training calls, we also sponsor weekly and monthly events for yourself and your guests. As an associate, you can get access to our beautiful multi-million-dollar web site, which becomes *your* site and allows you to sign up new members online.

How It Works

First become a member of Pre-Paid Legal Services, Inc., so you can experience the services firsthand. Then become an independent associate, working both for yourself and within this large organization. You are the boss, so you can make your own business as large or as small as you want it. When you join my group (go to www.shemin.com for details), we support you in whatever way we can.

You can easily start by selling individual memberships one on one, as I did in the beginning. Commissions start at about $75 per membership. For example, if you interest people through the brochure and they go to your web site, or you give them a tape or video and they sign up for the service, you will get a commission of about $75 per membership. That amount goes up once you sell a certain number of memberships. Please read the actual agreement on my web site (www.shemin.com).

You can go into mainly small- and medium-sized companies to enroll 20 to 100 people at a time. Pre-Paid Legal Services, Inc., is one of the hottest employee benefits going. Across the country, we are uncovering a huge demand for Pre-Paid Legal Services and we have penetrated only 1 to 2 percent of the market.

You can get paid for training and developing a sales force *and* make overrides on what they do, just like any other sales business does. Pre-Paid Legal Services has a sales commission plan similar to those of most finance and insurance companies in this country. You can make a great part-time or

(continued)

Continued

full-time income. Some people develop large national sales forces and make *overrides* that are substantial.

Questions and Answers

Q. What do you get for the fee you pay to be an associate?

A. When you pay the one-time fee of about $249, you get trained in the product and receive sales materials. You also get a home study course and access to a local fast-start training class.

Q. How well can you expect to do financially by going into Pre-Paid Legal Services, Inc., as a business?

A. Let me first give you a comparison. A friend of mine just bought one of the top franchises in the United States, a retail store. He spent $120,000 on that business. In his first year of operation, he plans to make between $10,000 and $20,000 working six days a week. He mortgaged his house and is $90,000 in debt, so you can see he is serious about the business. In the second year, he will make $30,000 to $40,000; in the third year, $50,000 to $80,000. In the fourth or fifth year, he might sell it and pocket $200,000.

Just as in most businesses, including real estate investing, most people who become involved do nothing. The people who do nothing are paid nothing; the people who do little are paid little; and those who do a lot reap commensurate rewards.

The investment for Pre-Paid Legal Services, Inc., is a one-time fee plus (in about 14 states) a fee of about $130 to get a license to sell. Personally, I think it is too low. If the fee to sell these services was $30,000, some serious people would still step forward.

If you come in for $249 and sell five memberships, you would bring in about $500. That puts you in the profit zone immediately. If you sell five to seven memberships a month for a year, you can earn trips to exotic locations and a car allowance of about $300 a month besides the commission.

I'm sold on this program both as a service and as another source of income. I encourage you to look into this today at www.shemin.com.

Please consult company brochures and contracts, because commissions, coverages, and bonuses may change.

Legal Shield

Maybe you feel that you get treated differently because of the way you look, the color of your skin, the car you drive. All of a sudden, Pre-Paid Legal Services, Inc., puts into your hands a legal shield for you and your family. If your teenagers, for example, get pulled over by the police, who want to question and detain them, and they show their membership card indicating they have immediate access to top attorneys, they might be treated differently.

I would not let any of my loved ones drive around without that legal shield, because we all have constitutional rights, even if we may not be aware of them. I highly respect this company and its chairman for creating this legal shield to make sure that everybody is treated fairly because of this access to top attorneys.

Business Advice

For your business, you can call and ask questions about incorporation procedures, LLCs, limited partnerships, real estate contracts, lease options, tenant problems, collection problems, credit problems, even divorce and bankruptcy problems.

If you would like more information about Pre-Paid Legal Services, Inc., go to my web site at www.shemin.com.

PREVENTIVE MAINTENANCE

Protecting yourself, your properties, and your investments is really a form of preventive maintenance. You hear that term used a lot in connection with physical health, but it's no less powerful a concept applied to all aspects of life, and certainly to real estate. When you take care to protect—in advance—all aspects of your new career, you stand to minimize significantly any associated problems and risks. Moreover, by putting protection systems in place, you ensure that when things do go wrong, you'll know how to handle them or whom to call to handle them for you.

And speaking of systems, the next and last chapter is a compilation of systems—guidelines, really—that serves as a review of all we've covered so far.

chapter 14

ensuring your success in real estate

The greatest things in the world have been done by those who systematized their work and organized their time.

—Orison Swett Marden

One thing that gets in the way of success as a real estate investor is what I call "being in our own way." We think too much; we worry too much. That's why we need systems for our real estate investment business. Systems take out the guesswork and confusion from the decision-making process.

You might fret, "Oh, no, a tenant called and can't pay the rent this month. What do I do?" Then you spend the next week stressing out, not taking any action. But if you have a policy in place that says, "The rent is due on the first of the month; it's late on the eleventh; we evict on the fifteenth or work out a payment plan in writing," you have no decisions to make.

By implementing systems, you reduce the amount of time you spend thinking and worrying. Some people go to their jobs every day at 8:00 A.M., make 10 phone calls from 8:00 to 9:00, and fill in 10 reports from 10:00 to 11:00. They know what they have to do—their company and every job has a system. You, too, can set up a "don't worry" system for your business of buying real estate without using your own capital or credit.

At McDonald's, the employees have a policy and procedures manual that lays out practically every detail: "Open bun, put burger on bun, put pickle on burger, close bun." Consequently, these employees have very few decisions to make. You can copy this model by writing a policy and procedures manual that frees you from making dozens of decisions every day.

As real estate investors, it's critical to build systems for success. Everything should be a system. Even getting properties without using your own money. When you call the bank and can't make a payment, the bank representatives don't say, "Oh my God, what do we do? Let's have meetings; let's worry about it. He said he lost his job and she said she's not feeling well. They're really nice, what do we do?" Instead of making up solutions as they go along, they follow their procedures.

robert's tip

To drastically change your life and your profitability, create a ritual: Take 30 minutes every Friday and review how you actually spent your time during the week. Record all of your activities and how long they took, and write down which activities made money for you. One week, for example, I had 82 meetings, was on the phone for 30 hours, and shopped for drywall for 4 hours at a store.

I estimate that most of us spend 70 to 80 percent of our time on activities that make absolutely no money and don't really help us. And yet we're busy and excited and stressed out. Take 30 minutes every Friday and review what you did the week before, then focus on spending your time on more profitable activities. If you do this, I predict you will drastically increase your productivity, your happiness, and your profitability. When I started doing that a few years ago, it changed how I did everything. I got rid of some businesses so I could focus on what was more fun and more profitable—and you need to do the same.

You don't have to make it up anymore; just develop and follow your own system and procedures, recording them in a policy and procedures manual. All successful businesses have a system. Set it up, operate it, and fine-tune your real estate investing like any successful business.

ESTABLISH AND FOLLOW GENERAL BUSINESS POLICIES AND PROCEDURES

Start by establishing some general business policies and procedures. Here are a number I have found effective:

- Return all phone calls within one business day. If people call in the morning, make sure their calls are returned by that afternoon. If they call late in the day, make sure they are called by the next business morning. The biggest frustration potential sellers, tenants, and buyers have is that no one calls them back. The average telemarketer can make anywhere from 20 to 60 calls an hour, so we can call everybody back within that business day, and so can you.

- Set a three-day repair guarantee. If we don't fix our tenants' repairs in three business days, we give them their daily rent back in cash. That shows we are serious about repairs and want to take care of our tenants.

- Touch all mail only once.

- Touch all paperwork only once. Like the mail, open it and immediately act upon it or put it where it needs to go.

- Pay all bills upon receipt.

- Have one folder for each property. Take a photograph of each property and place it in the folder.

- Always pay people bonuses if they do a good job. If we promise $500 to someone who bird-dogged a deal for us and we make a lot more than that, we pay them a bonus above the promised amount.

You can add to these policies and procedures as you go along, but I guarantee having them will cut down on your stress and worry.

GET ORGANIZED

Please do not operate your real estate business like I did the first two years, sticking Post-its on my car and on the side of my desk. Get organized from the start. Make sure your bookkeeping, accounting, banking, and filing systems are set up to do your real estate business.

These days, you can do most everything on the computer using Quickbooks. It's an inexpensive program with lots of different functions and accounts. It actually has a section set up for real estate to make your job easier.

You also want to open up one bank account for each of your real estate avenues of income. Do not commingle your funds. For example, if you have rental property, have a separate accounting system and dedicated bank account for it. If you do wholesaling and flipping, have those transactions in a separate entity with a separate accounting system and bank account. If you're out discounting mortgages, put that under a separate accounting system, separate filing system, and separate bank account.

Get someone who is proficient in bookkeeping or accounting to set up your system now. Real estate can be a lot of fun and profitable, but it also can be a tremendous amount of paperwork, especially as you start doing more and more deals.

FILE IDEAS

You should always keep files for each of your activities. Here are some recommendations:

- Keep a file for potential deals that you can go back through, and back through, and back through, with your property acquisition sheets.

- Keep a folder on each property with the address on the top and a picture.

- Keep all of your incoming and outgoing bills separate, so you know what to pay and what's going in and out.

- For every closing that you do, make sure you receive all the paperwork. Have a checklist so that you know you are getting the original filed closing statements, deeds, notes, and title insurance. Also make sure they give you amortization schedules, so you know what the loan balances are at all times of all the debt that you or your partners may have. Being organized now will help you tremendously in the future.

WRITE DOWN PLANS

Take all the notes for your action plans that you started writing and for the next several minutes, write down the actions and activities you'll do this week, next week, and the following weeks to find deals. Here are some key components of your plan.

Decide how much free time you have to put into real estate investing. You may have only five hours a week because you're busy, or you may want to pursue this full-time.

Decide how you're going to find deals. Run an ad, drive for dollars, go to auctions, go to the real estate association, hand out flyers, call Realtors, and so on.

Now make a one-week plan, a 30-day plan, a 60-day plan, and a 90-day plan. Over the next 90 days, consistently look for deals, set goals, and make offers. When you're looking for deals, write the following on the bottom of your data sheet: "My goal is to make 5 offers next week. The next week, I'm going to make 10 offers. The week after that, I'm going to make 20 offers."

use humor

An investor I was trying to close a deal with just wouldn't return my phone calls. He's busy, like everybody. I called him one day, left a message asking him to call me back, and he didn't. I called the next day. I called him 17 days in a row before he finally returned my phone call. I'm always polite. I never get upset. As a matter of fact, I use humor. After a few days, I said, "Look, obviously you're not calling me back; you might be on a three-week vacation; you might have been abducted by aliens and are unable to return my phone call; maybe you've been kidnapped and are tied up in a basement. Or you might be getting frustrated that I'm calling so much and don't ever want to talk to me. Call me and let me know which reason it is." After that message, he laughed and called me. That's why I recommend always being polite, but persistent. My policy and procedure is to call specific people every day until they call me back. What's your policy?

Write down your favorite one or two ways to buy property with no money down. Maybe you have perfect credit and are going to borrow money. Maybe you don't have any money or credit, and you want to wholesale, lease-option, and find a partner with money. Maybe you really love zero-financing opportunities and making full-price offers, so you focus on that.

Write down your answers to the following:

- How many deals would you like to do in the next 30 days, 60 days, 90 days? _____
- How many calls will you have to make on properties to find those deals? _____
- How much time will you spend doing it? _____
- How many properties would you like to have at the end of the year? Two years and three years from now? _____

_____   _____

Go to the mortgage company or bank and ask for preapproval so you'll know where you stand. Also, line up one or two partners with money and find a hard moneylender. You're going to need them, because even if you sell a property to other investors, they might need money, so you need to have sources. If you have zero money invested, your return is infinite.

FOCUS ON PROFIT

You may have thoughts like this: "I'm busy all week, and I know I'm really working hard, but I'm not making any money."

Or you may find an activity that is extremely lucrative for you. For instance, one year I wholesale-flipped more than 50 properties while doing other activities, including running a property management business. That kept me extremely busy . . . and stressed out. I had employees, an office, a lot of activity, a lot of stress. Money came in and money went out. But that management business made zero profit. I was focusing on being busy and doing things I was good at because I knew I was a good property manager. Chances are, you're good at many things, but you must focus on what you're *best* at—what makes your business profitable.

Track your activities and the time spent on them every day on a daily log worksheet, like the one shown here. Include your best estimate of your enjoyment and profitability for each activity.

ACTIVITY	TIME SPENT	ENJOYMENT FACTOR (1–10, WITH 10 BEING MOST)	PROFITABILITY FACTOR (1–10, WITH 10 BEING HIGHEST)
1.			
2.			
3.			
4.			
5.			
6.			
7.			
8.			
9.			
10.			

FIND GOOD DEALS AND MOTIVATED SELLERS

Focus on finding deals, because almost everything else you do in real estate is a waste of your precious time. Some of the activities—the paperwork, the repairs, the meetings with contractors, the property management—are necessary, but they're not moneymaking activities.

If you find a deal that's worth $600,000 for $400,000, you have several options to choose from: Do a lease option, flip it, fix it and sell it, rent it to make monthly income, and so on. What's most profitable is finding that deal. It may surprise you to know I've found a lot of deals spending only two to four hours a week looking. I have spent 20 to 30 hours looking for deals, making a ridiculous amount of money that would be unfit to print. But over time, I shifted from focusing on activities that kept me busy and stressed out to focusing on finding deals.

Finding a good deal in real estate is a numbers game. You have to look at a bunch of properties and talk to a lot of people to find a good or even great deal. Most successful investors use only one or two or three ways to find good deals. But I've shown you many ways to find them.

A good deal in real estate can be defined as a sale price of a *minimum* of 20 percent below what that property is worth in the retail market today, taking into account the cost of repairs. If a house is worth $100,000, and I can get it for $80,000 (which is a 20 percent discount) but it needs $20,000 worth of repairs, then it's not a good deal. If the $100,000 house can be purchased and repaired for $75,000, that's 75 cents on the dollar, or a 25 percent margin. In today's tight, competitive real estate market, a lot of deals are what I call "20 percenters," which are priced at least 20 percent below what they're worth. It's important to have a good-sized margin, because you could face more repairs than expected, or you could incur holding costs if it takes a long time to sell.

A good deal in real estate means you've found a motivated seller. Again and again, ask the question, "Why are you selling?" You waste your time trying to force a deal if the seller isn't pressured to sell because of a divorce, ill health, pending foreclosure, or whatever. Make it a win-win situation.

Let's say you could find a property worth $80,000 and pay $60,000. In southern California, we'd have to add some zeros, so let's say you bought a house worth $800,000 for $600,000.

To get those prices and make it worthwhile to buy as an investment, that property must have a motivated seller. Who are motivated sellers? People going through a divorce, having an estate sale, dealing with a foreclosure, being transferred out of state, and so on. Maybe they're older people who have to sell their home because it needs repairs and they don't want to do them.

Would lenders give you $600,000 to purchase a property worth $800,000? Probably. But if you can't get a loan from the bank, you can turn to a real estate partner

robert's tip

Why would people sell a property for less than it's worth? Because they find themselves in a tough situation. Or sometimes people simply do things that don't make sense. Why don't they wear their seat belts? Why don't they go to the gym? Why do they smoke cigarettes? Why do they drink too much? Don't waste time and energy trying to understand why.

with good credit or lots of money or to a hard moneylender or to another investor to lend you the funds. You could borrow the funds or maybe do owner's terms (i.e., the owner lends you the money so he or she can sell the property quickly). (By the way, if that owner doesn't use a 1031 tax-free exchange and resells for $600,000 the same property purchased 20 years ago for $100,000, he would pay $120,000 in taxes—almost 20 percent of that $600,000.)

Knowledge is power. Just by knowing that 1031 tax-free exchanges exist, you could help someone who qualifies save more than $100,000 in taxes. Perhaps you could work with a local accountant or real estate closing attorney who does 1031 exchanges and advertise for people who want to sell their investment properties without paying any capital gains taxes.

You can begin to see that there are ways to purchase property without using any of your own funds if you find the property to be a good enough value. Even if you don't have a lot of cash or great credit, if you find a property that's selling for 20 to 30 percent below its worth, someone will

 **think about it**

Rodney, a student of mine, found a one-bedroom penthouse condominium on the ocean in South Beach, Miami, Florida, through a real estate agent. The condo was incredible. It was listed for about $510,000, the fully appraised value. Rodney asked the Realtor why the seller was selling. She replied that the owner had six homes: one in Italy, one in New York, and several others around the world. He had not visited his condo in South Beach for more than two years and simply didn't want it anymore. Rodney negotiated and got the condo under contract for $430,000, with its expensive furniture included. He wholesaled, or flipped, the condo to another person within three weeks for $485,000, or $30,000 below its worth. Rodney made about $45,000 profit on this deal. He didn't buy it; he didn't use or borrow any money. Instead, he got paid for finding a good deal and making everyone happy. Why did the seller accept an offer for about $80,000 less than the condo was worth? Because he wanted to. He was so wealthy, it would be like throwing out some old shoes! Don't worry about his reasons; it doesn't make any difference. Just do it.

I suggest that you stop trying to figure out why people do the things they do. Focus instead on your own activity. Worry only about what you're doing. That will be enough to keep you busy.

put the word out

It pays to advertise. Here are a number of inexpensive ways to generate deals.

Flyers

Make flyers—and distribute lots of them. They might say, "We will pay cash for your house. Can close quickly. Call me first. We will buy your house. We will make an offer on every property." You want your phone to ring so you can find great deals.

Ads

Place an ad in your local newspaper that states, "We will buy houses. We will pay cash." Typically, these ads generate two to three calls a day and lead to about one deal a week. Is it worth $190 a week to run an ad? Yes, because one deal can be worth a lot.

Run your ad consistently and for a long time. This is critical. If you run it for three months to a year and the wording attracts attention, you will get calls and, eventually, good deals.

Direct Mail

Sending direct mail through the postal service usually gets a response rate of 1 to 2 percent, so do not expect a high-volume return for your efforts. However, if you mail a large quantity, you will get activity. Monitor the numbers carefully, and be consistent with your direct-mail campaign, so you know which mailings work well for you.

Door Hangers

When you come home at night, sometimes you see hanging on your door advertisements for carpet cleaning and pizza specials. You can use this idea and pay the same people to hand out your door hangers. Your message would read: "We pay cash for a house. Can close quickly. Do you know of any houses for sale that are a good deal? Call me. Referral fees paid."

Signs

Put signs in your targeted neighborhood on every corner and you will get calls. The largest real estate franchises attract their prospects by running billboards that say, "We will buy any house, ugly or pretty. We will pay cash. Call now." These signs generate lots of calls and the companies make tons of money.

Car Signs

I flew to Ohio one time to speak at a real estate association. I noticed the fellow who picked me up at the airport had put a big plastic sign on the

(continued)

Continued

side of his Jeep Cherokee that said, "We will pay cash for your house. Call me." I thought, "I don't like the way this ugly sign covers up a beautiful truck." Nonetheless, I asked Dennis if he got calls from this sign. He replied, "I get about five calls a week and one deal a month. I made about $8,000 on one of them last month and $25,000 on a fixer-upper." That ugly sign becomes a beautiful one when motivated sellers call you.

Co-op Advertising

You can partner with businesses that are already advertising through flyers, door hangers, even pizza boxes. Instead of advertising alone, you combine your efforts with others and spread your message farther for the same amount of money and time spent.

Think about all the people advertising on restaurant menus, on shopping carts, on street signs in your targeted neighborhoods. If you can cooperate with any of them, you will generate calls that can lead to deals.

My experience is that if you do not advertise, nothing will happen. And if you do advertise, something will happen.

An investor named John in Ohio owns more than 900 houses. Why does he have 900 houses while you and I do not? Because he places signs on park benches, on street corners, on pizza boxes. He prints and distributes flyers, door hangers, and business cards. This kind of advertising works where John is, and it will work where you live, too.

step in and either lend you the money or pay you for finding this good deal.

To find willing sellers, you could run ads and distribute flyers that say something like this: "Sell your property and pay zero taxes. Find out if you qualify. Call 888-302-8018, or visit our web site, www.shem-inrealestate.com." In the sidebar you'll find lots of other promotional ideas.

FIND GOOD BUYERS

Once you find good deals, you need to find good buyers. People often ask about my system for finding buyers, and I tell them it's very complicated. A few months ago, I sold 14 duplexes, a big investment for a potential investor. I found that investor by running an ad in the local newspaper. It cost me about $40 for one Sunday ad and generated about 30 calls from potential buyers. The fifth caller bought it, and I made a lot of money from that deal.

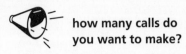

how many calls do you want to make?

Professional telemarketers can make 40 to 60 calls in an hour if they're focused and really going. So get focused: Spend at least three hours a week making phone calls. You won't connect with everyone. You'll get voice mail and busy signals. Some people won't call you back—as in any business. But if you were to call for three focused hours a week and could call only 30 people in an hour, you'd still reach between 50 and 100 of them. Over six months, how many people would you call—and how many potential deals would you find?

BUILD A DATABASE

Capture the names of everyone you meet for your database. If you have a computer, use ACT or a similar type of contact management program. If you don't have a computer, just keep a folder and write down every person who is a potential buyer: name, address, phone number, fax number, and e-mail address. Also, record what type of property these people would like to buy so that when you find a deal, you can look through your list and fax, e-mail, or call them. Every real estate agent, every mortgage person, every investor, every landlord, every landlady, every person you contact from newspaper ads—add to your list. You're setting up a system for finding buyers.

Most people who do well financially have connections and keep making more. Everyone you speak with should be listed in your contact database under one of the following categories:

1. Sellers of properties
2. Buyers of properties
3. Financers of properties and potential partners in your real estate business

FIND SOURCES OF MONEY

If you're serious about real estate and finding deals, you'll run out of money and need to involve people who have money. That's why you'll need systems for finding people with money.

Build a strong network of mortgage brokers, bankers, wealthy people, investors, retired investors, and other people with money. As a fallback, you can always run an ad in the paper to source these people.

GET HELP FROM EXPERTS

If you're not good at something, get help doing that, even paying your bills. By paying a bookkeeping service just about $100 a month, I ensure that all my books, records, and financial statements are clear and legible. At the end of the year, all my tax work is done because the bookkeeping or accounting firm has kept good records. You may want to consider doing the same. That frees you to find more deals and make more money. It is also liberating when a bank or partner needs a copy of your financial statements or balance sheets. You can find them easily, and they will be professionally done.

MANAGE YOUR TIME

If you are out finding good deals, your hourly rate will be in the hundreds, if not thousands, of dollars. Beware of spending lots of time on activities like dealing with contractors, driving to the paint-and-hardware store, taking tenant calls, trying to collect money, and running errands. These time-consuming, stressful, and nonproductive activities hurt your real estate investing business. Consider these ideas:

- Keep track of the amount of time you spend in half-hour or quarter-hour increments in your real estate business. Keep a daily log, a weekly log, and a monthly log. Every week, find out how you spend your time and what makes you the most money for the time spent. Determine what you enjoy the most, what you dislike, and what does not bring in dollars.

- If you spend 95 percent of your time on activities you don't like and that don't make you any money, increase the amount of time you spend on the activities that you like and that make you money.

- Hire someone to do the activities you do not like for about $15 an hour. Hire a courier service to pick up and deliver packages for about $10 or $12 a run. This saves me a couple of hours a day sitting in traffic and being stressed out. It also gives me more time to find good deals.

- Hire experienced managers to manage your property for 8 to 10 percent of rents collected. Then manage the managers, and make sure they do a good job.

- Get out of the contracting and repair business. Hire people to do it and manage them, or hire someone to manage them.

- Hire an administrative assistant or bring someone in as a quasi-partner to do bookkeeping, filing, phone answering, and so on. That will free you to make more money doing more deals.

- Track your deals. It is important to understand and track what one deal is worth to you. If you find one property and wholesale it for $8,000, it probably took only 5 to 15 hours to do that. Again, every week, review how you spend your time and what makes you money, and spend more time on the things that make you money.

One other important topic I want to cover when it comes to time management. Most likely, when you start out in a new business, particularly in real estate investing, you discover it's fun, exciting, and profitable. You may become addicted to it and find yourself working 60-hour weeks, even 80-hour weeks. And all of a sudden, you're working all the time. Your personal life, your family life, and your spiritual life begin to suffer.

Don't forget, the reason you started your business was to achieve financial freedom. Here are two important systems to use to ensure you won't overdo it.

Set Office Hours

You'll add to your enjoyment if you set office hours. Decide, if this is a part-time business, "I'm going to work Wednesday from 4:00 to 7:00, diligently and with focus, and I'm going to work Saturday from 1:00 to 5:00 or Sunday from 11:00 to 4:00." You'll find that you focus better and accomplish more when you have a finite amount of time to work. If you gave yourself seven days a week to work, you'd probably spread out whatever work had to be accomplished over those seven days. Whether you're a part-time or a full-time investor, set your office hours and keep them.

Delegate

Every business has multiple components, especially running your own real estate investing. Find out what you like to do, what you're good at,

robert's tip

Do this experiment. Give yourself, your children, or a friend a task and insist it has to be done within one week. How long do people take to get things finished? You'll find it takes them a full week. Do you remember when you finally sat down to write your term paper in high school? Yes, the night before your paper needed to be turned in. You'll likely find that people tend to do a job at the last minute and take only as much time as they have. Try it yourself.

then do those things yourself and hire others to do the things you don't like. Could you learn to change the brakes on your car? Change your oil? Even cut your own hair? You probably could figure out how to do these things, but you don't because you don't want to. It's stressful, it's a headache, you're not that good at it, and others are better equipped to do it than you, so you don't mind paying these specialists. Be careful when you get into real estate investing; you may try to do everything. "I'm going to paint, drywall, take out the garbage, do the bookkeeping and computer work, list the properties, write up all the papers, do the title searches, become an appraiser." The thought of doing all those jobs holds a lot of real estate investors back. Whatever tasks cause you headaches, simply hire other people to do them.

HAVE FUN AND REWARD YOURSELF

My goal (and your goal) is to have fun in real estate investing and make it profitable for years to come. That is why you want to develop a stellar reputation, to do what you say you will do when you do it. If you can't afford to do something, don't do it. If you put a contract in on a property, make sure you have enough information so you can close on it and not let others down. If you are not conscientious, you will gain a bad reputation and no one will want to do business with you.

For example, if you are wholesaling properties, make sure that you leave others who are involved enough room to make a good profit. If they make as much as or more than you, they will keep coming back. If you do not let them profit, they will be gone. Remember, two or three good clients can make you hundreds of thousands of dollars a year, every year, for dozens of years.

When you get paid after wholesaling a house or doing a no-money-down deal, take 10 percent of it and do something fun. Reward yourself. As business owners and real estate investors, we work, work, work, make, make, make, and we rarely reward ourselves. Get a massage, take a trip, go on a picnic, jump out of an airplane (with a parachute) . . . do something fun.

tools for running your real estate investment business

This appendix, divided into two sections—"Legal Forms" and "Business Forms and Procedures"—includes excellent tools to keep you organized and within legal guidelines for your real estate investing business. It includes forms and contract samples used by real estate investors to streamline their business. This selection is not meant to be comprehensive, but rather a sampling of commonly used forms that have been developed and refined over the years. In addition, the last two items in this appendix—"Formulating a Winning Strategy" and "My Plan"—are procedures that will help you assess your strengths and goals and then proceed with a plan.

If you would like to receive a full set of forms in a CD-ROM format, or if you would like to sign up for advanced seminars in real estate investing, landlording, and asset protection, please call 888-302-8018, or visit www.shemin.com for full details.

LIST OF FORMS

Forms and contracts, as well as guidelines for success, are included in this appendix.

1. Legal Forms
    - Agreement for Deed
    - Agreement of Trust
    - Contract to Purchase Real Estate
    - Contract of Sale
    - Quit Claim Deed
    - Mortgage Purchase Agreement
    - Offer to Assign and Sell a Note and Deed of Trust
    - Land Installment Contract
    - Warranty Deed to Trustee
    - Promissory Note
    - Power of Attorney

2. Sample Forms and Procedures
    - Property Acquisition Worksheet
    - Hiring Contractors
    - Rehab Worksheet
    - Procedures for Contractors
    - Loan Qualification Worksheet
    - Information Sheet for Notes (Loans)
    - Lease-Option Prospect Qualification Form
    - Letter to Potential Investors to Sell a Property
    - Letter to Insurer to Put Owner's Name on Policy
    - Property Business Plan Example
    - Formulating a Winning Strategy
    - My Plan

LEGAL FORMS

Agreement for Deed

THIS AGREEMENT FOR DEED made this _____ day of A.D., 20___, BY AND BETWEEN _____ of the County of _____, State of _____, hereinafter referred to as SELLER, and _____ hereinafter referred to as PURCHASER.

WITNESSETH, that provided the said purchasers shall first make the payments and perform the covenants hereinafter set forth on their part to be made and performed, the said sellers covenant and agree to and will by good and sufficient warranty deed, convey, and assure to the said purchasers, their heirs, and assigns forever in fee simple, free, and clear of all encumbrances, the following described land situated in _____ County, _____ to wit:

The purchase price of said land is $_____, of which the purchasers have herewith paid to the sellers the sum of $_____, and the purchasers agree to pay to the sellers the balance, to wit: the principal sum of _____ dollars, together with interest on so much of said principal sum as remains from time to time outstanding and unpaid at the rate of per centrum from until paid; said principal and interest to be payable in payments consecutive on the _____ day of each and every month beginning with the day of _____, 20___; said installments to be applied first to interest and balance to principal. If any payment is not received within ___ days of due date, there shall be a late charge of _____% added. The purchasers may prepay any part of the principal sum hereof in multiples of $_____ on any installment payment date, but any such prepayment shall not relieve the purchasers from making the payment of the installment then due and any subsequent installment provided hereby unless at the time of such prepayment the purchasers pay all sums unpaid hereon.

The PURCHASERS covenant and agree as follows: (a) to pay all taxes, fines, and assessments levied or assessed on said land subsequent to December 31, 20__, as and when the same respectively become due and shall exhibit to sellers immediately after such payment the official receipts therefore; (b) to place and continuously keep on the building now or hereafter situated on said land fire and extended-coverage insurance in the usual standard policy form in a sum not less than $_____ in such company or companies as may be approved by the sellers, and said policies shall be delivered up and held by the sellers and contain the usual clauses making said policies payable to the sellers as their interest may appear, and in the event any sum of money becomes payable under such policies, the sellers shall have the right to receive and apply the sum on account of the indebtedness secured hereby; (c) to permit, commit, or suffer no waste, impairment, or deterioration of said property or any part thereof; (d) to at all times keep and maintain the buildings and improvements on said land in a good and tenantable state of repair and condition.

Time is of the essence in this agreement, and in the event of any breach of this agreement or default on the part of the purchasers of any kind whatsoever, the sellers may without notice to the purchasers exercise the following options: (a) to terminate this agreement and retain all sums of money theretofore paid by the purchasers as liquidated damages and/or the reasonable rental value of said land, and to render said premises and take possession thereof fully and to all intents and purposes as if the purchasers had no interest in said property whatsoever, or (b) to accelerate all sums of money secured by this agreement whether due by the literal terms hereof or not, and to foreclose this agreement in accordance with the rules of practice applicable to vendors' liens, in which event the purchasers agree to pay all costs of collection and foreclosure, including a reasonable attorney's fee.

The words *seller, sellers, purchaser,* and *purchasers,* whether in the singular or plural as the case may be wherever used herein, shall be taken to mean and include the singular, if only one, and plural, jointly and severally, if more than one, and their respective heirs, assigns, and legal representatives; and, that the word *their* taken to mean his, her, or its wherever the context hereof so implies or admits.

IN WITNESS WHEREOF, the parties hereto have hereunto set their hands and seals the day and year first above written.

_____   _____
Witness   SELLER

_____
Witness

_____   _____
Witness   PURCHASER

_____
Witness

STATE OF: _____

COUNTY OF: _____

Before me personally appeared _____ to me well known and known to me to be the person(s) described in and who executed the foregoing instrument, and acknowledged to and before me that he executed said instrument for the purpose therein expressed.

WITNESS my hand seal, and official seal this ____ day of _____, 20___.

Notary Public: _____

State of: _____

My Commission Expires: _____

STATE OF: _____

COUNTY OF: _____

Before me personally appeared _____ to me well known and known to me to be the person(s) described in and who executed the foregoing instrument, and acknowledged to and before me that he executed said instrument for the purpose therein expressed.

WITNESS my hand seal, and official seal this ____ day of _____, 20___.

Notary Public: _____

State of: _____

My Commission Expires: _____

This instrument was prepared by: _____

Agreement of Trust

THIS AGREEMENT AND DECLARATION OF TRUST is made and entered into this ____ day of _____, 20___, by and between _____, as Grantors and Beneficiary (hereinafter referred to as the *Beneficiary* or *Beneficiaries,* whether one or more, which designation shall include all successors in interest of any beneficiary), and _____ whose address is _____ (hereinafter referred to as the *Trustee,* which designation shall include all successor trustees).

IT IS MUTUALLY AGREED AS FOLLOWS:

1. *Trust Property.*   The Beneficiary is about to convey or cause to be conveyed to the Trustee by deed, absolute in form, the property described in the attached *Exhibit A,* which said property shall be held by the Trustee, in trust, for the following uses and purposes, under the terms of this Agreement and shall be hereinafter referred to as the *Trust Property.*

2. *Consideration.*   No consideration has been paid by Trustee for such conveyance. The conveyance will be accepted and will be held by Trustee subject to all existing encumbrances, easements, restrictions, or other clouds or claims against the title thereto, whether the same are of record or otherwise. The property will be held on the trusts, terms, and conditions and for the purposes hereinafter set forth, until the whole of the trust estate is conveyed, free of this trust, as hereinafter provided.

3. *Beneficiary.*   The person(s) named in the attached *Exhibit B* are the Beneficiary(ies) of this Trust (referred to as *Beneficiary* or *Beneficiaries*), and as such, shall be entitled to all of the earnings, avails, and proceeds of the Trust Property according to their interests set opposite their respective names.

4. *Interests.*   The interests of the Beneficiary shall consist solely of the following rights respecting the Trust Property:

   a. The right to direct the Trustee to convey or otherwise deal with the title to the Trust Property as hereinafter set out.

   b. The right to manage and control the Trust Property.

   c. The right to receive the proceeds and avails from the rental, sale, mortgage, or other disposition of the Trust Property.

The foregoing rights shall be deemed to be personal property and may be assigned and otherwise transferred as such. No beneficiary shall have any legal or equitable right, title, or interest as realty, in or to any real estate held in trust under this Agreement, or the right to require partition of that real estate, but shall have only the rights, as personally set out above, and the death of a beneficiary shall not terminate this Trust or in any manner affect the powers of the Trustee.

1. *Power of Trustee.*

    a. With the consent of the Beneficiary, the Trustee shall have authority to issue notes or bonds and to secure the payment of the same by mortgaging the whole or any part of the Trust Property; to borrow money, giving notes therefore signed by him in his capacity as Trustee; to invest such part of the capital and the profits therefrom and the proceeds of the sale of bonds and notes in such real estate, equities in real estate, and mortgages in real estate in the United States of America, as he may deem advisable.

    b. With the consent of the Beneficiary, the Trustee shall have the authority to hold the legal title to all of the Trust Property, and shall have the exclusive management and control of the property as if he were the absolute owner thereof, and the Trustee is hereby given full power to do all things and perform all acts which in his judgment are necessary and proper for the protection of the Trust Property and for the interest of the Beneficiary in the property of the Trust, subject to the restrictions, terms, and conditions herein set forth.

    c. Without prejudice to the general powers conferred on the Trustee hereunder, it is hereby declared that the Trustee shall have the following powers, with the consent of the Beneficiary:

        (1) To purchase any real property for the Trust at such times and on such terms as may seem advisable; to assume mortgages upon the property.

        (2) To sell at public auction or private sale, to barter, to exchange, or to otherwise dispose of any part, or the whole of the Trust Property which may from time to time form part of the Trust estate, subject to such restrictions and for such consideration for cash and/or for credit, and generally upon such terms and conditions as may seem judicious, to secure payment upon any loan or loans of the Trust, by mortgage with or without power of sale, and to include such provisions, terms, and conditions as may seem desirable.

        (3) To rent or lease the whole or any part of the Trust Property for long or short terms, but not for terms exceeding the term of the Trust then remaining.

(4) To repair, alter, tear down, add to, or erect any building or buildings upon land belonging to the Trust; to fill, grade, drain, improve, and otherwise develop any land belonging to the Trust; to carry on, operate, or manage any building, apartment house, or hotel belonging to the Trust.

d. To make, execute, acknowledge, and deliver all deeds, releases, mortgages, leases, contracts, agreements, instruments, and other obligations of whatsoever nature relating to the Trust Property, and generally to have full power to do all things and perform all acts necessary to make the instruments proper and legal.

e. To collect notes, obligations, dividends, and all other payments that may be due and payable to the Trust; to deposit the proceeds thereof, as well as any other monies from whatsoever source they may be derived, in any suitable bank or depository, and to draw the same from time to time for the purposes herein provided.

f. To pay all lawful taxes and assessments and the necessary expenses of the Trust; to employ such of officers, brokers, engineers, architects, carpenters, contractors, agents, counsel, and such other persons as may seem expedient, to designate their duties and fix their compensation; to fix a reasonable compensation for their own services to the Trust, as organizers thereof.

g. To represent the Trust and the Beneficiary in all suits and legal proceedings relating to the Trust Property in any court of law of equity, or before any other bodies or tribunals; to begin suits and to prosecute them to final judgment or decree; to compromise claims or suits, and to submit the same to arbitration when, in their judgment, such course is necessary or proper.

h. To arrange, pay for, and keep in force in the name and for the benefit of the Trustee, such insurance as the Trustee may deem advisable, in such companies, in such amounts, and against such risks as determined necessary by the Trustee.

2. *Duties of Trustee.*   It shall be the duty of the Trustee, in addition to the other duties herein imposed upon him:

a. To keep a careful and complete record of all the beneficial interests in the Trust Property with the name and residence of the person or persons owning such beneficial interest, and such other items as they may deem of importance or as may be required by the Beneficiary.

b. To keep careful and accurate books showing the receipts and disbursements of the Trust and also of the Trust Property, and such other items as he may deem of importance or as the Beneficiary hereunder may require.

c. To keep books of the Trust open to the inspection of the Beneficiary at such reasonable times at the main office of the Trust as they may appoint.

d. To furnish the Beneficiary at special meetings, at which the same shall be requested, a careful, accurate, written report of their transactions as Trustees hereunder, of the financial standing of the Trust, and of such other information concerning the affairs of the Trust as they shall request.

e. To sell the Trust Property and distribute the proceeds therefrom:

(1) If any property shall remain in trust under this Agreement for a term which exceeds that allowed under applicable state law, the Trustee forthwith shall sell same at public sale after a reasonable public advertisement and reasonable notice to the Beneficiary and, after deducting its reasonable fees and expenses, the Trustee shall divide the proceeds of the sale among the then Beneficiaries as their interests may then appear, without any direction or consent whatsoever, or

(2) To transfer, set over, convey, and deliver to all the then Beneficiaries of this Trust their respective, undivided interests in any nondivisible assets, or

(3) To transfer, set over, and deliver all of the assets of the Trust to its then Beneficiaries, in their respective proportionate shares, at any time when the assets of the Trust consist solely of cash.

3. *Compensation of Trustee.* The Beneficiary jointly and severally agrees that the Trustee shall receive reasonable compensation monthly for his services as Trustee hereunder.

a. *Liability of Trustee.* The Trustee and his successor as Trustee shall not be required to give a bond, and each Trustee shall be liable only for his own acts and then only as a result of his own gross negligence or bad faith.

b. *Removal of Trustee.* The Beneficiary shall have the power to remove a Trustee from his office or appoint a successor to succeed him.

c. *Resignation and Successor.*

(1) Any Trustee may resign his office with thirty (30) days' written notice to Beneficiary, and Beneficiary shall proceed to

elect a new Trustee to take the place of the Trustee who had resigned, but the resignation shall not take effect until a certificate thereof, signed, sealed, and acknowledged by the new Trustee and a certificate of the election of the new Trustee, signed and sworn to by the Beneficiary and containing an acceptance of the office, signed and acknowledged by the new Trustee, shall have been procured in a form which is acceptable for recording in the registries of deeds of all the counties in which properties held under this instrument are situated. If the Beneficiary shall fail to elect a new Trustee within thirty (30) days after the resignation, then the Trustee may petition any appropriate court in this state to accept his resignation and appoint a new Trustee.

(2) Any vacancy in the office of Trustee, whether arising from death or from any other cause not herein provided for, shall be filled within thirty (30) days from the date of the vacancy, and the Beneficiary shall proceed to elect a new Trustee to fill the vacancy, and immediately thereafter shall cause to be prepared a certificate of the election containing an acceptance of the office, signed, sealed, and acknowledged by the new Trustee, which shall be in a form acceptable for recording in the registries of deeds of all the counties in which properties held under this instrument are situated.

(3) Whenever a new Trustee shall have been elected or appointed to the office of Trustee and shall have assumed the duties of office, he shall succeed to the title of all the properties of the Trust and shall have all the powers and be subject to all the restrictions granted to or imposed upon the Trustee by this agreement, and every Trustee shall have the powers, rights, and interests regarding the Trust Property, and shall be subject to the same restrictions and duties as the original Trustee, except as the same shall have been modified by amendment, as herein provided for.

(4) Notwithstanding any such resignation, the Trustee shall continue to have a lien on the Trust Property for all costs, expenses, and attorney's fees incurred and for said Trustee's reasonable compensation.

4. *Objects and Purposes of Trust.*   The objects and purposes of this Trust shall be to hold title to the Trust Property and to protect and conserve it until its sale or other disposition or liquidation. The Trustee shall not undertake any activity not strictly necessary to the attainment of the foregoing objects and purposes, nor shall the Trustee transact business within the meaning of applicable state law, or any other law, nor shall this Agreement be deemed to be, or create or evidence the existence of a corporation, de facto or de jure, or a Massachusetts Trust, or any other type of business trust, or an association in the nature of a corporation, or a partnership or joint venture by or between the Trustee and the Beneficiary, or by or between the Beneficiary.

a. *Exculpation.*   The Trustee shall have no power to bind the Beneficiary personally and, in every written contract he may enter into, reference shall be made to this declaration; and any person or corporation contracting with the Trustee, as well as any beneficiary, shall look to the funds and the Trust Property for payment under such contract, or for the payment of any debt, mortgage, judgment, or decree, or for any money that may otherwise become due or payable, whether by reason or failure of the Trustee to perform the contract, or for any other reason, and neither the Trustee nor the Beneficiary shall be liable personally therefore.

b. *Dealings with Trustee.*   No party dealing with the Trustee in relation to the Trust Property in any manner whatsoever, and, without limiting the foregoing, no party to whom the property or any part of it or any interest in it shall be conveyed, contracted to be sold, leased, or mortgaged by the Trustee, shall be obliged to see to the application of any purchase money, rent, or money borrowed or otherwise advanced on the property; to see that the terms of this Trust Agreement have been complied with; to inquire into the authority, necessity, or expediency of any act of the Trustee, or be privileged to inquire into any of the terms of this Trust Agreement. Every deed, mortgage, lease, or other instrument executed by the Trustee in relation to the Trust Property shall be conclusive evidence in favor of every person claiming any right, title, or interest under the Trust that at the time of its delivery, the Trust created under this Agreement was in full force and effect; and that instrument was executed in accordance with the terms and conditions of this agreement and all its amendments, if any, and is binding upon all Beneficiaries under it; that the Trustee was duly authorized and empowered to execute and deliver every such instrument; if a conveyance has been made to a successor or successors in trust, that the successor or successors have been appointed properly and are vested fully with all the title, estate, rights, powers, duties, and obligations of its, his, or their predecessor in Trust.

c. *Recording of Agreement.*   This Agreement shall not be placed on record in the county in which the Trust Property is situated, or elsewhere, but if it is so recorded, that recording shall not be considered as notice of the rights of any person under this Agreement derogatory to the title of powers of the Trustee.

d. *Name of Trustee.*   The name of the Trustee shall not be used by the Beneficiary in connection with any advertising or other publicity whatsoever without the written consent of the Trustee.

e. *Income Tax Returns.*   The Trustee shall be obligated to file any income tax returns with respect to the Trust, as required by law, and the Beneficiaries individually shall report and pay their share of income taxes on the earnings and avails of the Trust Property or growing out of their interest under this Trust.

f. *Assignment.*   The interest of a Beneficiary, or any part of that interest, may be transferred only by a written assignment executed in duplicate and delivered to the Trustee. The Trustee shall note his acceptance on the original and duplicate original of the assignment retaining the original and delivering the duplicate original to the assignee as and for his or her evidence of ownership of a beneficial interest under this Agreement. No assignment of any interest under this Agreement, other than by operation of law, that is not so executed, delivered, and accepted shall be valid without the written approval of all of the other Beneficiaries, if any, who possess the power of direction. No person who is vested with the power of direction, but who is not a Beneficiary under this Agreement, shall assign that power without the written consent of all of the Beneficiaries.

g. *Individual Liability of Trustee.*   The Trustee shall not be required, in dealing with the Trust Property or in otherwise acting under this Agreement, to enter into any individual contract or other individual obligation whatsoever; nor to make himself individually liable to pay or incur the payment of any damages, attorneys' fees, fines, penalties, forfeitures, costs, charges, or other sums of money whatsoever. The Trustee shall have no individual liability or obligation whatsoever arising from its ownership, as Trustee, of the legal title to the Trust Property, or with respect to any act done or contract entered into or indebtedness incurred by him in dealing with the Trust Property or in otherwise acting under this Agreement, except only as far as the Trust Property and any trust funds in the actual possession of the Trustee shall be applicable to the payment and discharge of that liability or obligation.

h. *Reimbursement and Indemnification of Trustee.* If the Trustee shall pay or incur any liability to pay any money on account of this Trust, or incur any liability to pay any money on account of being made a party to any litigation as a result of holding title to the Trust Property or otherwise in connection with this Trust, whether because of breach of contract, injury to person or property, fines or penalties under any law, or otherwise, the Beneficiaries, jointly and severally agree that on demand they will pay to the Trustee, with interest at the maximum rate allowed under the laws of the State of Tennessee per annum, all such payments made or liabilities incurred by the Trustee, together with its expenses, including reasonable attorneys' fees, and that they will indemnify and hold the Trustee harmless of and from any and all payments made or liabilities incurred by him for any reason whatsoever as a result of this Agreement; and all amounts so paid by the Trustee, as well as his compensation under this Agreement, shall constitute a lien on the Trust Property. The Trustee shall not be required to convey or otherwise deal with Trust Property as long as any money is due to the Trustee under this Agreement; nor shall the Trustee be required to advance or pay out any money on account of this Trust or to prosecute or defend any legal proceedings involving this Trust or any property or interest under this Agreement unless he shall be furnished with sufficient funds or be indemnified to his satisfaction.

(1) *Entire Agreement.* This Agreement contains the entire understanding between the parties and may be amended, revoked, or terminated only by written agreement signed by the Trustee and all of the Beneficiaries.

(2) *Governing Law.* This Agreement, and all transactions contemplated hereby, shall be governed by, construed, and enforced in accordance with the laws of the State of _____ applicable to contracts executed and performed in _____. The parties waive any right to a trial by jury and agree to submit to the personal jurisdiction and venue of a court of subject matter jurisdiction location in _____ County, State of _____. In the event that litigation results from or arises out of the agreement or the performance thereof, the parties agree to reimburse the prevailing party's reasonable attorney's fees, court costs, and all other expenses, whether or not taxable by the court as costs, in addition to any other relief to which the prevailing party may be entitled. In such event, no action shall be entertained by said court or any court of competent jurisdiction if filed more than one year subsequent to the date the cause(s) of action actually accrued regardless of whether damages were otherwise, as of said time, calculable.

(3) *Binding Effect.*   The terms and conditions of this agreement shall inure to the benefit of and be binding upon any successor trustee under it, as well as upon the executors, administrators, heirs, assigns, and all other successors-interest of the Beneficiaries.

(4) *Trustee's Liability to Beneficiaries.*   The Trustee shall be liable to the Beneficiaries for the value of their respective beneficial interests only to the extent of the property held in trust by him hereunder, and the Beneficiaries shall enforce such liability only against the trust property and not against the Trustee personally.

(5) *Annual Statements.*   There shall be no annual meeting of the Beneficiaries, but the Trustee shall prepare an annual report of their receipts and disbursements for the preceding fiscal year, which fiscal year shall coincide with the calendar year, and a copy of the report shall be sent by mail to the Beneficiaries not later than February 28 of each year.

(6) *Termination.*   This trust may terminate at any time by a majority of the Beneficiaries and within thirty (30) days' written notice of termination delivered to the Trustee, the Trustee shall execute any and all documents necessary to vest fee simple marketable title to any and all trust property in the Beneficiary.

In Witness Whereof, the parties hereto have executed this agreement as of the day and year first above written.

Beneficiary:

_____

Trustee:

_____

STATE OF: _____
COUNTY OF: _____

Personally appeared before me, _____, a Notary Public in and for the State and County aforesaid, _____, the within named bargainer, with whom I am personally acquainted (or proved to me on the basis of satisfactory evidence), and who acknowledged that he executed the foregoing instrument for the purposes therein contained.

WITNESS my hand and seal at office, on this _____ day of _____, 20___.

Notary Public: _____

State of: _____

My Commission Expires: _____

STATE OF: _____

COUNTY OF: _____

Personally appeared before me, _____, a Notary Public in and for the State and County aforesaid, _____, the within-named bargainer, with whom I am personally acquainted (or proved to me on the basis of satisfactory evidence), and who acknowledged that he executed the foregoing instrument for the purposes therein contained.

WITNESS my hand and seal at office, on this _____ day of _____, 20___.

Notary Public: _____

State of: _____

My Commission Expires: _____

EXHIBIT A
Legal Description

EXHIBIT B
Beneficiaries and Their Interests
Name and Address   *% of Interest*

_____   _____

_____   _____

100%

Contract to Purchase Real Estate

I/We offer to purchase from Seller the following described real estate, together with all improvements thereon and all appurtenant rights, located at:

Address: _____ City: _____

County: _____ State: _____ Zip: _____

The purchase price is to be $_____ payable as follows:

The conditions of the Purchase are as follows:

Subject to review, inspection, and written approval of my financial partner.

Purchaser shall have the right to assign his/her interest in this contract prior to escrow. Seller agrees to allow purchaser to show property to prospective partners and clients prior to closing.

Is there an Addendum to this contract? Yes _____ No _____

Is this deal "All Cash" or "Terms"? "All Cash" _____ "Terms" _____

Possession is to be given on or before _____.

Seller agrees to pay all Taxes and Assessments up to and including the month of _____, 20____.

Closing costs shall be paid by: Seller _____ Purchaser _____ Split _____

Closing date shall be on or before _____, 20____, with title to the previously described real estate to be conveyed by Warranty Deed with release of dower. Title is to be free, clear, and unencumbered, free of building orders, subject to zoning regulations of record, and except easements and restrictions of record.

This offer, when accepted, comprises the entire agreement of Purchaser and Seller, and it is agreed that no other representation or agreements have been made or relied upon.

This offer is to remain open for acceptance until _____.

Date: _____   Date: _____

Seller: _____   Purchaser: _____

Seller: _____   Purchaser: _____

Contract of Sale

THIS CONTRACT of sale made this _____ day of _____ 20___, by and between _____, hereinafter called SELLER, and _____, hereinafter called BUYER.

WITNESSETH: That the seller in considerations of the sum of _____ Dollars as earnest money and in part payment of the purchase price has this day sold and does hereby agree to convey by a good and valid warranty deed to said buyer, or to such person as he may in writing direct the following described real estate in _____ County, in the state of _____, to wit:

CONSIDERATION: Buyer agrees to purchase said real estate and to pay therefore the sum of _____ Dollars, upon the following terms: $_____ cash, balance.

MISCELLANEOUS CONDITIONS:

TITLE INSURANCE: The _____ or his agent, at seller's expense, agrees to make application to the _____ for Title Insurance on the aforementioned property, and if after examination by this Company the title is found insurable, the buyer hereby agrees to accept a title Policy issued by said Company in its usual form and to comply with this contract WITHIN 10 DAYS after receiving a report on the title, and it is agreed that such report shall be conclusive evidence of good title subject to the exceptions therein stated, otherwise the earnest money is to be refunded.

Should the buyer default in the performance of this contract on his part at the time and in the manner specified, then at seller's option the earnest money shall be forfeited as liquidated damages. But such forfeiture shall not prevent suit for the specific performance of this contract.

In the event of default in the terms of this contract for any reason on the part of the seller and in the event it becomes necessary, due to any fault of the sellers that the earnest money herein shown previously, must be returned to the buyer, then the seller shall be liable to the agent herein for the full commission set out in this contract.

The words SELLER and BUYER when used in this contract shall be construed as plural whenever the number of parties to this contract so requires.

SELLER ACKNOWLEDGMENT: Seller acknowledges that buyer is a licensed Real Estate Broker and is purchasing said property for rental or resale.

ADJUSTMENTS TO BE MADE AT TIME OF CLOSING:

(1) Seller's Escrow Deposits to be _____

(2) Taxes for Current Year _____

(3) Seller's Fire Insurance to be _____

(4) Existing Leases or Rents _____

Possession to be _____

Conveyance to be subject to existing Building Restrictions and/or Zoning Ordinances _____. Seller to bear risk of hazard loss to date of deed.

Purchaser: _____

Seller: _____

Purchaser: _____

Seller: _____

Deed Property to: _____

Quit Claim Deed

ADDRESS New Owners:	SEND TAX BILLS to:	MAP PARCEL number:
Name Street Address or Route Number City, State, Zip	Name Street Address or Route Number City, State, Zip	

FOR AND IN CONSIDERATION of One Dollar ($1.00), cash in hand paid, the receipt of which is hereby acknowledged, I _____, by these presents do hereby quit claim and convey unto _____ successors and assigns, all _____ rights, title, and interest in and to the following, described tract of land:

STATE OF: _____

COUNTY OF: _____

The actual consideration for this transfer is $_____. Subscribed and sworn to before me this the _____ day of _____, 20____.

Notary Public: _____

State of: _____

My commission expires: _____
    (Affix Seal)

Said property is conveyed subject to such limitations, restrictions, and encumbrances as may affect the premises.

Witness _____ hand _____ this ____ day of _____, 20___, the corporate party, if any, having caused its name to be signed hereto by its duly authorized officers on said day and date.

_____   _____

Mortgage Purchase Agreement

This agreement is made and entered into this _____ day of _____, 20___, by and between _____ located at _____, hereinafter referred to as the SELLER and _____, located at _____, hereinafter referred to as the BUYER.

WHEREAS, SELLER holds and owns a certain note in the face amount of $_____ bearing interest at the rate of ____ percent per annum with a remaining unpaid principal balance on the date hereof of approximately $_____, I secured by a mortgage or trust deed on certain real estate within the County of _____, State of _____, the street address of which property is:

_____

_____

_____

known as the MORTGAGE, a copy of the note and mortgage are attached hereto.

NOW, THEREFORE, SELLER and BUYER do hereby agree as follows:

1. SELLER agrees to sell _____ payments at a/an payment amount of $_____ and a balloon payment, if applicable, of $_____, due _____ for $_____ to the BUYER or any purchaser(s) secured by BUYER.

2. SELLER warrants that the representations with respect to the MORT-GAGE are correct on the date hereof, that prompt notice to BUYER will be given of any default in the MORTGAGE, and that title to the property serving as security for repayment of the note is marketable except for the lien created by the MORTGAGE and any senior mort-gages or deeds of trust to wit:
    FURTHER, SELLER warrants that the property serving as security for repayment of the note will appraise, by an independent appraiser selected by BUYER, at a value acceptable to Buyer. Should the prop-erty serving as security for the repayment of the note not appraise at this value or higher, SELLER agrees to reimburse BUYER for the appraisal fee plus any other documented out-of-pocket expenses, and this agreement shall terminate.

3. Should SELLER refuse to consummate the closing of this said sale, then SELLER agrees to reimburse BUYER for all documented out-of-

pocket expenses including, but not limited to, appraisals, title searches, and credit checks. A $100.00 administration fee will also be due.

4. In the event the documents reflect information different than that represented by SELLER, the payor's creditworthiness is found to be unsatisfactory, title defects are of record, or other circumstances reflect unfavorably on the purchase, BUYER may terminate this agreement.

5. BUYER represents that BUYER does, from time to time but without obligation to do so, purchase mortgages and deeds of trust for his own account. SELLER acknowledges receipt of this disclosure that BUYER may purchase the mortgage, for his own account, to hold or resell. SELLER agrees that any purchase and subsequent resale of the MORTGAGE shall not in any way constitute a breach of any fiduciary duty owed by BUYER to SELLER.

6. A facsimile of this document shall be deemed and considered as an original, binding, and enforceable document.

Dated as listed previously.

Seller: _____

Seller: _____

Buyer: _____

Offer to Assign and Sell a Note and Deed of Trust

FOR VALUABLE CONSIDERATION, I (we), the undersigned _____ (SELLER), offer and agree to assign, convey, and sell to _____ (BUYER), his successors, or assigns, the note and deed of trust held by the undersigned on which the PAYOR is: (Name, address, and phone of Payor) for _____ DOLLARS to be paid as follows: (Terms and schedule of purchase payment)

The said deed of trust is recorded in _____ County, State of _____, in the Registry of Deeds, BOOK _____, PAGE _____, and dated _____.

Property address is _____.

The approximate principal balance as of _____ on said note and deed of trust is $_____, and the monthly payment is $_____ per month. There are _____ payments remaining. Next payment is due on _____.

The PAYOR has been late in making payments, and the payments are now months in arrears.

I (we) fully warrant that I have disclosed all information of which a prudent purchaser should be aware.

The BUYER, his successors, or assigns shall have until _____ to exercise and accept this offer to assign and sell. Acceptance shall be by written notice to the seller, with the settlement to be held on or before at _____.

At settlement, seller will provide, in addition to the ORIGINAL NOTE and the ORIGINAL DEED OF TRUST, the following:

Seller is advised that this is a binding contract to assign and to sell the preceding described note and deed of trust, and if it is not fully understood, legal counsel should be consulted before signing.

Dated: _____

_____   _____
ASSIGNOR   ASSIGNOR

Land Installment Contract

THIS AGREEMENT is made and entered into by and between _____, hereinafter called the *Vendor*, and _____, hereinafter called the *Vendee*.

WITNESSETH: The Vendor, for himself, his heirs, and assigns, does hereby agree to sell to the Vendee, his heirs, and assigns the following described real estate together with all appurtenances, rights, privileges, and easements, and all buildings and fixtures in their present condition located upon said property.

1. Contract Price, Method of Payment, Interest Rate

In consideration whereof, the Vendee agrees to purchase the aforementioned property for the sum of _____ Dollars ($_____), payable as follows:

The sum of $_____ as down payment at the time of execution of the Land Installment Contract, the receipt of which is hereby acknowledged, leaving a principal balance owed by Vendee of $_____, together with interest on the unpaid balance payable in consecutive monthly installments of $_____, beginning on the _____ day of _____, 20___, and on the _____ day of each and every month thereafter until said balance and interest are paid in full, or until the _____ day of whichever event occurs first. The interest on the unpaid balance due hereon shall be ___ (%) percent per annum computed monthly, in accordance with a _____-month amortization schedule during the life of this Contract.

Payments shall be credited first to the interest, and the remainder to the principal or other sums due Vendor. The total amount of this obligation, both principal and interest, unpaid after making any such Application of payments as herein receipted, shall be the interest-bearing principal amount of this obligation for the next succeeding interest computation period. If any payment is not received within ____ days of payment date, there shall be a late charge of (____%) percent assessed. The Vendee may pay the entire purchase price on this contract without prepayment penalty. The monthly installments shall be payable as directed by the Vendor herein.

2. Encumbrances

Said real estate is presently subject to a mortgage, and the Vendor shall not place any additional mortgage on the premises without the written permission of the Vendee. In the event the Vendor should become delinquent in payments on the mortgage, the Vendee may pay the same and credit said payment to the contract price.

3. Evidence of Title

The Vendor shall be required to provide an abstract or guarantee of title, statement of title, title insurance, or such other evidence of title.

4. Recording of Contract

The Vendor shall cause a copy of this contract to be recorded in the _____ County Recorder's Office within a period of twenty (20) days after the execution of this Contract by the parties hereto.

5. Real Estate Taxes

Real estate taxes shall be prorated to the date of the closing using the short-term method of tax proration being those becoming due and payable on _____, 20___. When the real estate taxes become due and payable, the Vendee shall pay the same directly to the _____ County Treasurer and provide proof of payment to the Vendor.

6. Insurance and Maintenance

The Vendee shall keep the premises insured for at least _____ thousand Dollars ($_____) against fire and extended coverage for the benefit of both parties, as their interest may appear, and provide a copy of the said policy to the Vendor or any mortgage.

The Vendee shall keep the building in a good state of repair at the Vendee's expense. At such time as the Vendor inspects the premises and finds that repairs are necessary, Vendor shall request that these repairs be made within sixty (60) days at the Vendee's expense.

The Vendee has inspected the premises constituting the subject matter of this Land Installment Contract, and no representations have been made to the Vendee by the Vendor in regard to the condition of said premises; it is agreed that the said premises are being sold to the Vendee as the same now exists and that the Vendor shall have no obligation to do or furnish anything toward the improvement of said premises. Vendor shall furnish a clear termite report at Vendor's expense prior to executing this contract. If the property has live infestation of wood-destroying organisms, Vendor will pay costs of treatment and repair damages caused by same. If Vendor elects not to do so, Vendee may elect to waive Vendor's responsibility and proceed, or Vendee may elect not to proceed with this contract.

7. Possession

The Vendee shall be given possession of the earlier described premises at Contract execution and shall thereafter have and hold the same subject to the provisions for default hereinafter set forth.

8. Delivery of Deed

Upon full payment of this contract, Vendor shall issue a General Warranty deed to the Vendee, free of all encumbrances except as otherwise set forth. In addition, Vendee reserves the right to convert this contract into a note and mortgage and receive a Warranty Deed to Vendee or assigns from Vendor, anytime the following conditions have been met by the Vendee:

1. At least 20 percent of the purchase price has been paid to Vendor.
2. Vendee is willing to pay all the costs of title transfer and document preparations.

The note and mortgage will bear the same terms as this contract for the remaining balance.

9. Default by Vendee

If an installment payment to be made by the Vendee under the terms of this Land Contract is not paid by the Vendee when due or within two (2) installments thereafter, the entire unpaid balance shall become due and collectable at the election of the Vendor, and the Vendor shall be entitled to all the remedies provided for by the laws of this state and/or to do any other remedies and/or relief now or hereafter provided for by law to such Vendor; and in the event of the breach of this contract and any other respect by the Vendee, Vendor shall be entitled to all relief now or hereinafter provided for by the laws of this state.

Waiver by the Vendor of a default or a number of defaults in the performance hereof by the Vendee shall not be construed as a waiver of any default, no matter how similar.

10. General Provisions

There are no known pending orders issued by any governmental authority with respect to this property other than those spelled out in the Land Installment Contract prior to closing date for execution of the contract.

It is agreed that this Land Installment Contract shall be binding upon each of the parties, their administrators, executors, legal representatives, heirs, and assigns.

IN WITNESS WHEREOF, the parties have set their hands this _____ day of _____, 20___.

Signed in the presence of: Vendor:

_____   _____

_____   _____

Signed in the presence of: Vendee:

_____   _____

_____   _____

STATE OF: _____

COUNTY OF: _____

On this ____ day of _____, 20___, before me, a Notary Public in and for said county and state, personally came, _____ Vendor(s) and _____ Vendee(s) in the foregoing Land Installment Contract, and acknowledged the signing thereof to be their voluntary act and deed.

WITNESS my official signature and seal on the last day mentioned previously.

Notary Public _____

State of: _____

My commission expires: _____

Warranty Deed to Trustee

The Grantor(s) _____ of the County of _____ and the State of _____ for and in consideration _____ Dollars, and other good and valuable considerations in hand paid, conveys, grants, bargains, sells, aliens, remises, releases, confirms, and warrants under provisions of Section _____.

Unto _____ as Trustee and not personally under the provisions of a trust agreement dated the ____ day of _____, 20___, known as Trust Number _____, the following described real estate in the County of _____, State of _____, to wit:

Together with all the tenements, hereditaments, and appurtenances thereto, belonging or in anywise appertaining.

To have and to hold the said premises in fee simple forever, with the appurtenances attached thereto upon the trust and for the uses and purposes herein and in said Trust Agreement set forth.

Full power and authority granted to said Trustee, with respect to the said premises or any part of it, and at any time or times, to subdivide said premises or any part thereof, to dedicate parks, streets, highways, or alleys, and to vacate any subdivision or part thereof, and to resubdivide said property as often as desired, to contract to sell, to grant options to purchase, to sell on any terms to convey either with or without consideration, to donate, to mortgage, to pledge, or to otherwise encumber said property, or any part thereof, to lease said property, or any part, from time to time, in possession or reversion by leases to commence now or later and upon any terms and for any period or periods of time and to renew or extend leases upon any terms and for any period or periods of time and to amend, change, or modify and the terms and provisions thereof at any time hereafter, to contract to make leases and to grant options to lease and options to renew leases and options to purchase the whole or any part of the reversion and to contract respecting the manner of fixing the amount of future renters to partition or to exchange the said property or any part thereof for other real or personal property, to grant easements or changes of any kind, to release, convey, or assign any right, title, or interest in or about easement appurtenant to said premises or any part, and to deal with said property and every part thereof in all other ways and for such other considerations as it would be lawful for any person owning the same to deal with the same, whether similar to or different from the ways heretofore specified, at any time or times hereafter.

In no case shall any party dealing with the said trustee in relation to said premises, to whom said premises or any part thereof shall be conveyed, contracted to be sold, leased or mortgaged by said trustee, be obliged to see to the application of any purchase money, rent, or money borrowed or advanced on said premises, or be obliged to see that the terms of this trust have been complied with, or be obliged to inquire into the necessity or expediency of any act of said trustee, or be obliged or privileged to inquire into any terms of said trust agreement; and every deed, mortgage, lease, or other instrument executed by said trustee in relation to said real estate shall be conclusive evidence in favor of every person relying upon or claiming under such conveyance, lease, or other instrument (a) that at the same time of delivery thereof, the Trust created by this Indenture and by said Trust Agreement was in full force and effect; (b) that such conveyance or other instrument was executed in full accordance if the trust's constitutions and limitations contained herein and thereunder trust agreement or in some amendment thereof and binding upon all beneficiaries thereunder; and (c) that said Trustee was duly authorized and empowered to execute and deliver every such deed, trust deed, lease, mortgage, and other instrument.

The interest of each and every beneficiary hereunder and of all persons claiming under them or any of them shall be only in the earning, avails, and proceeds arising from the sale or other disposition of said real estate, and such interest is hereby declared to be personal property. No beneficiary hereunder shall have any title or interest, legal or equitable, in or to said real estate as such, but only an interest in the earnings, avails and proceeds thereof as aforesaid.

And the grantor hereby covenants with said grantee that the grantor is lawfully seized of said land in fee simple, that the grantor has good right and lawful authority to sell and convey said land and will defend the same against the lawful claims of any persons whomsoever, and that the said land is free of all encumbrances, except taxes accruing subsequent to December 31.

In witness whereof, the said grantor has hereunto set their hands and seals this _____ day of _____, 20___.

Signed, sealed, and delivered in our presence:

_____   _____
                                 Seal

_____   _____
                                 Seal

State of _____
County of _____

I hereby certify that on this day, before me, an officer duly authorized in the State aforesaid to take acknowledgments, personally appeared _____ to me known as the person(s) described in and who executed the foregoing Instrument and _____ acknowledged before me that he executed the same.

Witness my hand and official seal in the County and State aforesaid this _____ day of _____, 20___.

Notary Public: _____

State of _____

My Commission Expires: _____

Promissory Note

$_____   Dated: _____

Principal Amount: _____ State of: _____

FOR VALUE RECEIVED, the undersigned hereby jointly and severally promise to pay to the order of _____, the sum of _____ Dollars ($_____), together with interest thereon at the rate of _____ percent per annum on the unpaid balance. Said sum shall be paid in the manner following:

All payments shall be first applied to interest and the balance to principal. This note may be prepaid, at any time, in whole or in part, without penalty. All prepayments shall be applied in reverse order of maturity.

This note shall at the option of any holder hereof be immediately due and payable upon the failure to make any payment due hereunder within _____ days of its due date.

In the event this note shall be in default, and placed with an attorney for collection, then the undersigned agree to pay all reasonable attorney fees and costs of collection. Payments not made within five (5) days of due date shall be subject to a late charge of _____ percent of said payment. All payments hereunder shall be made to such address as may from time to time be designated by any holder hereof.

The undersigned and all other parties to this note, whether as endorsers, guarantors, or sureties, agree to remain fully bound hereunder until this note shall be fully paid and waive demand, presentment, and protest and all notices thereto and further agree to remain bound, notwithstanding any extension, renewal, modification, waiver, or other indulgence by any holder or upon the discharge or release of any obligor hereunder or to this note or upon the exchange, substitution, or release of any collateral granted as security for this note. No modification or indulgence by any hereof shall be binding unless in writing; any indulgence on any one occasion shall not be an indulgence for any other or future occasion. Any modification or change of terms hereunder granted by any holder hereof, shall be valid and binding upon each of the undersigned, notwithstanding the acknowledgment of any of the undersigned, and each of the undersigned does hereby irrevocably grant to each of the others a power of attorney to enter into any such modification on their behalf. The rights of any holder hereof shall be cumulative and not necessarily successive. This note shall take effect as a sealed instrument and shall be construed, governed, and enforced in accordance with the laws of the State first appearing at the head of this note. The undersigned hereby execute this note as principals and not as sureties.

Signed in the presence of:

_____   _____

_____   _____

GUARANTEE

We the undersigned jointly and severally guarantee the prompt and punctual payment of all monies due under the aforesaid now and agree to remain bound until fully paid.

Signed in the presence of:

_____   _____

_____   _____

Power of Attorney

KNOW ALL MEN BY THESE PRESENTS, that as principal (the "Principal") I, _____ of _____, have made, constitute, and appoint _____ as my true and lawful attorney ("Attorney"). Attorney is authorized in Attorney's absolute discretion from time to time and at any time with respect to any property, real or personal, at any time owned or held by me and without authorization of any court and in addition to any other rights, powers, or authority granted by any other provision of this power of attorney or by statute or general rules of law (and whether I am mentally incompetent, physically or mentally disabled, or incapable of managing my property and income), with full power of substitution, as follows:

1. To do and perform all and every act, deed, matter, and thing whatsoever in and about my estate, property, and affairs as fully and effectually to all intents and purposes as I might or could do in my own proper person, if personally present, the specifically enumerated powers described hereafter being in aid and exemplification of the full, complete, and general power herein granted and not in limitation or definition thereof.

2. To demand, sue for, and receive all debts, moneys, securities of money, goods, chattels, legacies, or other personal property to which I am now or may hereafter become entitled, or which are now or may become due, owing or payable to me from any person or persons whomsoever, and in my name to give effectual receipts and discharges for the same.

3. To borrow from time to time such sums of money and upon such terms as the said attorney may think expedient for or in relation to any of the purposes or objects aforesaid, or for any other purpose, upon the security of any of my property, whether real or personal, and for such purposes to give and execute open or unsecured notes and acknowledge mortgages or trust deeds with such powers and provisions as they may think proper, as well as such notes or bonds as it is necessary or proper to use therewith.

4. In my name, and as my act and deed, to sign, seal, acknowledge, and deliver all such leases and agreements as shall be requisite, or as my said attorney shall deem necessary or proper in the care and management of my estate; and to receive and collect all the rents that may be payable to me, and in my name to sign effectual receipts for the same.

5. To manage and superintend all of my real property whosesoever situates and found and to erect, pull down, and repair houses or other buildings,

or machinery or otherwise improve any of the premises, and to insure the buildings against damage by fire and windstorm.

6. To subdivide, develop real property to public use or to make or obtain the vacation of plats and adjust boundaries, to adjust differences in valuation on exchange or partition by giving or receiving consideration, and to dedicate easements to public use without consideration.

7. To make, draw, sign, or endorse in my name any checks, drafts, bills of exchange, or promissory notes in which I shall be interested or concerned, or which shall be requisite in or about my business.

8. To sell and dispose of such shares of stock as I now hold or may hereafter hold in any business corporation, or any bonds or securities of the United States or any state, municipal corporation, or private company, and to receive the consideration money for the sale thereof, and for me and in my name to transfer such shares, bonds, or securities to the purchaser or purchasers thereof.

9. To vote in person or by proxy upon any item of security or property owned by me; to agree to the reorganization, merger, or consolidation of any corporation whose stock is owned by me, and to unite, in their discretion, with other owners of similar property in carrying out any plan, making any change, giving any assent, and paying any sums of money affecting such securities or property, and, generally, to exercise in respect thereof the same rights and powers as are or may be lawfully exercised by persons owning similar property in their own right, and incident thereto, to accept in exchange for such stock or securities or other property, other stock, securities, or property, whether legal investments or not, in such reorganized or new corporation.

10. To invest and reinvest all or any part of my property in any property and undivided interests in property, wherever located, including bonds; debentures; notes, secured or unsecured; stocks of corporations regardless of class; interests in limited partnerships; real estate or any interest in any real estate, whether productive at the time of investment or not; interests in trusts; investment trusts, whether of the open and/or closed fund types; and participation in common, collective, or pooled trust funds or annuity contracts without being limited by any statute or rule of law concerning investments by fiduciaries.

11. To purchase for my benefit and in my behalf United States Government bonds, redeemable at par in payment of United States estate taxes imposed at my death upon my estate.

12. To obtain entry to and enter any lockbox in any bank or trust company wherein I may have leased or rented same, and to place therein my

papers, instruments, bonds, securities, or other property belonging to me or to remove any such papers, instruments, bonds, securities, or other property therefrom.

13. To bargain, sell, grant, and convey to such person or persons, and for such sum or sums of money or other consideration or considerations as my said attorney shall deem most for my advantage and profit, any and all of my property, real, personal, or mixed, whosesoever situate and found; to make all necessary deeds and conveyances thereof, with such covenants, warranties, and assurances as my said attorney shall deem expedient; to sign, seal, acknowledge, and deliver the same; to accept and receive the sum or sums of money or other consideration or considerations which shall be coming to me on account of such sale or sales.

14. To commence, prosecute, or enforce, or to defend, answer, or oppose, all actions or other legal proceedings touching any of the matters aforesaid, or any other matters in which I am or may hereafter be interested or concerned; and also, if it shall seem best, to compromise, refer to arbitration, or submit to judgment in any such action or proceeding.

15. To adjust, settle, compromise, or submit to arbitration any accounts, debts, claims and demands, disputes, and matters, touching any of the matters aforesaid, or any other matters that are now subsisting or may hereafter arise between me and any other person or persons or between my said attorney or any other person or persons.

16. To appoint and employ counsel, agents, servants, or other persons, at such salary or for such compensation as my said attorney may think proper, and to dismiss or discharge them and appoint or employ others in their place and stead.

17. To sign and execute in my name and as my act and deed all state and federal income tax returns, both preliminary and final, and to appear for me and represent me before the Treasury Department in connection with any matter involving federal taxes for any year whatsoever, in which I am a party, giving my said attorney full power to do everything whatsoever requisite and necessary to be done in the premises and to receive refund checks, to execute waivers of the Statute of Limitations, and to execute closing agreements, as fully as the undersigned might do if done in his own capacity, with full power of substitution and revocation, at any time subsequent to the date hereof and prior to the revocation hereof.

18. To make gifts of property, both real and personal, to my children (including Attorney), grandchildren and their spouses, or any trusts created for their benefit, provided, however, that no single gift during

any calendar year shall exceed the Federal Gift Tax Annual Exclusion then in effect for such year (or twice such amount if my spouse consents to having such gift treated as made one-half by her pursuant to Section 2513 of the Internal Revenue Code, as amended). For the purposes of this limitation, a gift in trust shall be deemed a gift to each of the beneficiaries.

19. To employ and compensate medical personnel including physicians, surgeons, dentists, medical specialists, nurses, and paramedical assistants deemed by Attorney needful for the proper care, custody, and control of my person and to do so without liability for any neglect, omission, misconduct, or the fault of any such physician or other medical personnel, provided such physician or other medical personnel were selected and retained with reasonable care, and to dismiss any such persons at any time, with or without cause.

20. To authorize any and all kinds of medical procedures and treatment including, but not limited to, medication, therapy, surgical procedures, and dental care, and to consent to all such treatment, medication, or procedures where such consent is required; to obtain the use of medical equipment, devices, or other equipment and devices deemed by Attorney needful for proper care, custody, and control of my person and to do so without liability for any neglect, omission, misconduct, or fault with respect to such medical treatment or other matters authorized herein.

In connection with the exercise of the powers herein described, Attorney is fully authorized and empowered to perform any other acts or things necessary, appropriate, or incidental thereto, with the same validity and effect as if I were personally present, competent, and personally exercised the powers myself. All acts lawfully done by Attorney hereunder during any period of my disability or mental incompetence shall have the same effect and inure to the benefit of and bind me and my heirs, devisees, legatees, and personal representatives as if I were mentally competent and not disabled. The powers herein conferred may be exercised by Attorney alone and the signature or act of Attorney on my behalf may be accepted by third persons as fully authorized by me and with the same force and effect as if done under my hand and seal and as if I were present in person, acting on my own behalf and competent. No person who may act in reliance upon the representations of Attorney for the scope of authority granted to Attorney shall incur any liability to me or to my estate as a result of permitting Attorney to exercise any power, nor shall any person dealing with Attorney be responsible to determine or insure the proper application of funds or property.

My mental or physical debility subsequent to my execution of the within power of attorney shall not revoke said power, which shall remain in full force and effect notwithstanding said mental or physical debility.

These presents shall extend to and be obligatory upon the executors, administrator, legal representatives, and successors, respectively, of the parties hereto.

IN TESTIMONY WHEREOF, I have hereunto affixed my signature this the day of _____, 20___.

STATE OF: _____

COUNTY OF: _____

On this _____ day of _____, 20___, before me, a Notary Public in and for said State and County, duly commissioned and qualified, personally appeared, to me known to be the person described in and who executed the foregoing instrument, and acknowledged that he executed the same as his own free act and deed.

WITNESS my hand and Notarial Seal at office the day and year first previously written.

Notary Public: _____

State of: _____

My Commission Expires: _____

SAMPLE FORMS AND PROCEDURES

Property Acquisition Worksheet

ADDRESS: _____

Estimated sales price after fix-up $_____

Down payment	
Closing costs	
Commission	
Appraisal	
Termite	
Miscellaneous	
Total expense to buy	
Rehab budget	
Cost overruns ($\pm 10\%$)	
Total rehab costs	
Payments for _____ months	
Property tax	
Insurance	
Total holding costs (+ your time and cost of your capital)	
Sale closing costs	
Commission	
Advertising, telemarketing	
Total sales costs	
$ Mortgage payoffs	
Total sales price	
Expense to buy	
Total rehab costs	
Total holding costs	
Total sales cost	

Your profit = $_____.

Hiring Contractors

Policy and Procedures

1. All proposed work to be performed for COMPANY will be submitted by written bid prior to any work being performed.

2. All part-time workers or bidders hired by COMPANY are independent subcontractors and are responsible for their own insurance and tax requirements. No worker or bidder shall hold COMPANY and Investment Corp. liable for any claims arising from any cause on any job. The liability for each job shall be the sole responsibility of the bidder alone.

3. NO check will be issued to any worker upon demand. Paid-on-completion jobs will be paid by check—AFTER inspection, after presentation of a proper invoice, within five (5) working days by mail.

4. NO checks will be mailed without an invoice.

5. NO checks will be written to walk-ins on demand.

6. Inspections are as follows—**NO EXCEPTIONS:**
   - *Roof.*   AFTER first significant rainfall or Metro Codes.*
   - *Electrical.*   AFTER final inspection and white tag from Metro Codes.
   - *Plumbing.*   AFTER full inspection of both supply and drainpipes and all fixtures or Metro Codes if applicable.
   - *HVAC.*   AFTER five days of continuous operation or verification of proper permit and subsequent final by Metro Codes.
   - *Hauling/trash disposal.*   AFTER dump receipts and invoice(s) are furnished.

7. All invoices should be mailed to COMPANY or left in the mailbox at COMPANY ADDRESS.

8. All calls from workers concerning the job or payment for work completed should be made during normal business hours, Monday through Friday, unless other instructions are given.

9. NO draws or advancements of any kind will be made to any worker for any reason other than those agreed on in a bid or other arrangement in writing—**NO EXCEPTIONS.**

DO NOT WALK IN AND REQUEST A CHECK—ALL CHECKS WILL BE MAILED.

*__Metro Codes inspection means:__ Cleared and released on their computers and the appropriate utility.

10. No tools will be furnished by COMPANY to any worker. Should an exception be made for an emergency, the worker is to be completely responsible for the tool(s). Should they be lost or damaged, COMPANY will deduct the amount necessary to replace the tool(s) from the worker's paycheck.

11. ALL BIDS must include a start date, estimate of time to complete, and a finish date. ALL BIDDERS must adjust their schedules to finish ON TIME. Work not performed within the bidder's own agreed schedule will be penalized at a rate of 5 percent (5%) per day of the total bid until completion. THIS WILL BE ENFORCED!

12. Any bidder who pulls off in the middle of a job WILL BE LIABLE for any difference in his bid and what it costs COMPANY to finish the job, plus the 5% per day penalty until the job is restarted with a suitable replacement.

13. Any bidder who agrees to perform work for COMPANY will NOT be allowed to subcontract the work to someone else without the written permission of COMPANY. The bidder is to be on the job site to perform the work HIMSELF and oversee his helpers.

14. Should any bidder hire helpers, they shall be the sole responsibility of the bidder, and he alone assumes all liability for them.

15. All work performed by bidder shall be in a quality workmanlike manner. The use of substandard materials, fewer materials than considered normal, or any attempt to cover up poor workmanship or inferior materials will result in immediate termination of the bidder—ON THE SPOT.

16. Any dispute over quality or workmanship will be resolved by the use of a for-hire independent inspectors' licensed contractor who is an expert in the category of the dispute, or a Metro Codes inspector.

17. The use, possession, presence, or the obvious effects of the use of any drugs or alcohol on any job site for COMPANY will be cause for IMMEDIATE TERMINATION—**NO EXCEPTIONS!**

18. Should any worker or bidder cause any damage to any part of the job site while performing their work, COMPANY will have the damage repaired and deduct that amount from the worker's paycheck.

THE FOLLOWING INFORMATION MUST BE COMPLETED BEFORE ANY BID IS CONSIDERED OR ACCEPTED OR ANY WORK IS PERFORMED:

1. Bidder's name:
2. Driver's license:

3. State:

4. Date of birth:

5. SS#:

6. Car license:

7. Make and model of car:

8. Phone number:

9. Current address:

10. One reference: Name: _____ Ph. #: _____

I have read this entire agreement and agree to all conditions. I understand and will abide by the preceding rules.

I understand and agree to all pay schedules, inspection procedures, and penalties for late work or noncompletion.

I understand that I am, alone, responsible for all taxes, insurance, and liabilities for myself and anyone I hire.

I will not hold COMPANY or any property owner responsible for any damages or liabilities on this job.

I understand that I cannot perform any work that is not bid in writing—and accepted in writing.

I understand that I cannot perform any work until this agreement is filled out completely and signed.

This is the only agreement between myself and COMPANY—there are no others—either implied, oral, or written.

Worker or Bidder: _____

Date: _____

Rehab Worksheet

1. CASH OUT OF POCKET	
Down payment	
Closing costs	
Appraisal	
Termite letter	
Survey	
Title insurance	
Miscellaneous	
TOTAL	
2. COST OF REHAB	
Flooring	
Painting	
Roofing	
Windows/screens	
Kitchen (e.g., faucets, cabinets)	
Bathroom (e.g., vanity, sink, tub)	
Bedrooms	
Decorations (e.g., ceiling fans, brass)	
Doors	
Foundation	
Fireplace	
Plumbing	
Insulation	
Subtotal: Total multiplied by a 15% repair cost overrun	
TOTAL	
3. ESTIMATED HOLDING COSTS	
No. of months × mortgage	
+ Insurance	
+ Taxes	
+ Utilities	
TOTAL	

4.	**ESTIMATED SELLING COSTS (following rehab)**	
	Closing costs	
	Attorneys' fees	
	Document/transfer	
	Taxes	
	Commissions	
	TOTAL	
5.	**TOTAL ESTIMATED. ACQUISITION, REHAB, HOLDING, and SELLING COSTS** (Add totals from 1, 2, 3, and 4)	
5a.	Plus (+) mortgage balance payoff	
6.	**TOTAL COST OF PROPERTY** (Add lines 5 and 5a)	
7.	**TOTAL PROJECTED SELLING PRICE** (following rehab)	
8.	**TOTAL PROFIT** (Subtract line 6 from line 7)	

Procedures for Contractors

There are no exceptions to the following policies and procedures:

- All contracts must be in writing and as detailed as possible.

- No checks will be issued without written contracts and invoices.

- Regarding draws, a maximum of one-third (⅓) of the total bid will be given up front to cover materials. The balance will not be paid until all work is complete. Absolutely complete. If one doorknob is loose or one sink has a small leak, the balance will not be paid.

- The balance will not be paid until all of the contractor's trash is removed.

- Service calls will not be paid until they are completed and verified by the tenant that they are complete.

- Contractor will give a date for the completion of a job. If the job is not complete, then the landlord loses money by not being able to rent out the property. Therefore, a $50.00 per day penalty will be deducted from the contractor's final draw for each day, including weekends, that the job is not done.

- On houses for Section 8, 20 percent of the total will be held back until the unit passes the Section 8 inspection.

- A $25 bonus will be paid for units that pass the Section 8 inspection the first time.

- Contractor will guarantee work for six months.

- Contractor must show proof of workers' compensation insurance. If not, the premiums will be deducted from the cost of the job and paid by the owner or property manager.

- All contractors must sign and agree to this contractor's agreement and attached agreement regarding liability and contractor's status as a contractor and not an employee.

OWNER MANAGER   CONTRACTOR

_____   _____

Loan Qualification Worksheet

The following worksheet will allow you to calculate the mortgage loan amount for which you qualify.

Maximum debt allowed

Stable monthly income	$_____
(Multiply by 0.28)	×28%
Maximum monthly housing expense	$_____
Stable monthly income	$_____
(Multiply by 0.36)	×36%

Maximum monthly housing expense

Plus other obligations	$_____

Monthly housing expense		Total monthly expenses	
Principal + interest	$_____	Total housing	$_____
Real estate taxes	$_____	Installment debt	$_____
Insurance premium	$_____	Revolving charges	$_____
Homeowner's		Alimony, etc.	$_____
association	$_____		
Other	$_____		
Total	$_____	Total	$_____

Compare actual to maximum expenses allowed. Actual expenses should not exceed the maximum allowed. These qualifications are the standard current guidelines used by most lenders in your area.

Information Sheet for Notes (Loans)

Holder: _____

Date: _____

Name: _____

Address: _____

Phone: _____ Source: _____

Note (Original) (Now) (First)

  Balance: (PV)

  Interest rate: (I)

  Payment amount: (PMT)

  Term: (N)

  Balloons: (FV)

  Present loan constant %:

  Creation date:

  Number of payments remaining:

  Why holder is selling:

  Seller needs: $_____ (YTM) _____% How soon? _____

Property

  Address: _____

  Property type: _____ Age: _____

Condition: _____

  Sale price $: _____

  Down payment $: _____

LTV ratio %: _____ Payor occupied? _____

Documents from seller (copies)

  Title policy and report

  Appraisal report

  Deed of trust (mortgage)

  Senior liens

Settlement sheet

  Deed

Fire/liability policy: _____

Appointment

  Date:

  Time:

Location: _____

Offered (or next step in the process): _____

Agreed contract purchase price: $_____

Settlement date: _____

Closer: _____ Phone number: _____

Settlement location: _____

Additional information: _____

Lease-Option Prospect Qualification Form

Name   Date/Time

Phone   Regarding Rating

Second Applicant's Name   Other Applicants   Pets

Are you looking to rent or own?

Have you seen the house? Y or N

Where do you live now?   How long there?

Is it a house or apartment?

How much do you pay now?

Have you ever been late with your payment?

Have you ever been evicted?

Is your landlord aware that you will be moving?

Employer/Position

How long there?   Gross salary?

Spouse Employer/Position

How long there?   Gross salary?

How is your credit?   How is your spouse's credit?

When can you move in?

What is the most you can pay per month?

How much money do you have to put down on your new home?

Can you pay extra per month to build up a down payment?

We know the bank requires this, and you won't ever be able to buy if we don't work out a down payment plan.

Tax return

We want you to succeed in having your own home!

Letter to Potential Investors to Sell a Property

Note: You can try a number of versions of this sample offer geared to any number of different types of investors (e.g., real estate club members, nonprofits).

Dear _____,

I'm writing to urge you to take immediate action on a wonderful opportunity that just became available. Here's what it's all about: I have a piece of property that I've purchased recently, that almost any astute, no-nonsense investor would find an exceptional value. I have completely rehabilitated the house and would welcome your inspecting any structural portion or mechanical system of the property. There are no serious defects, and the asking price is well below normal market value.

It is my opinion that, over any number of years of ownership, this property is going to give someone peace of mind knowing it is a sound financial investment. I will give you a call in the next few days to see if you have an interest. If you want even more prompt action, my telephone number is _____. Or, if you would like, I have prepared a fact sheet on this property and will send it to you upon request.

If I can be of help to you in answering any questions you might have regarding this property, please call me. I will also include a bit of information about the work that we do in the area, the people we help, and the solutions we provide for individuals and nonprofit organizations.

By the way, I realize that you may not know me, but I am familiar with your community. As a member of the community, I should tell you this: The kind of relationships I am seeking, whether you have an interest in this property or not, is a long and enduring one. I really only want to sell you something that meets your precise needs.

The fact is, from time to time, I'd be happy simply to show you some of the unique properties I uncover in the marketplace that go unrecognized. Of course, I won't be offended if you buy from someone else. Actually, I may advise you against certain properties, even though it might be in my interest to do otherwise.

It is the long-term relationship that meets the test of time that I want to maintain. I can also assure you I will make available my best deals even if we never make contact again. I will make sure that the only situations I show you are those that are in your self-interest. I don't want you to ever make any errors and, frankly, I don't want to make any myself.

Sincerely,

Your Name

Follow-Up to Letter

Here's a suggested telescript for following up: "Mr. Jones, this is Sally Robbins. I am calling you to see if you received the letter I sent regarding a piece of property that is now available and whether you had any questions about it. I am on a tight schedule but would be delighted to take the time to answer any questions that you might have regarding the property."

Letter to Insurer to Put Owner's Name on Policy

Note: If you have an interest in a property, make sure you are named as an insured party. Here is an example of a letter you might write to the company that insures your property, or make sure the seller writes and sends it on your behalf.

(date)

XYZ Insurance Company
123 Jump Street
Anytown, VA

    RE: Policy Number _____
    Policy Name _____
    Property Owner _____
    Property Address _____

Dear Sirs:

You are hereby notified that an interest in a deed of trust secured by the above property has been purchased by _____.

Please add the below-named as beneficiary to the above-described policy as loss payee.

Should there be a lapse of insurance due to a nonpayment of the premium, please notify the note purchaser at the address below.

Sincerely,

Signed: (seller of the note)

Information about the purchaser (new beneficiary):

Name:
Mailing address:
Telephone:

Property Business Plan Example

Greenwood Court Project

Brief Description

Sixteen brick duplexes, each containing two two-bedroom, one-bath apartments of about 850 square feet, located in a nice area of East Nashville. All but about eight units are rented for between $355.00 and $400.00 per month. Over 90 percent of the tenants are on the Section 8 program, which means the government pays all or most of the rent. All of the tenants and rents qualify as low or very low income according to the Department of Housing and Urban Development.

The vacancies are due to the fact that they are the last ones to be rehabilitated. All of the other units have just gone through a major rehabilitation. The units are located in a court that dead-ends, enabling the owner to control the area.

Long-Term Plan

To rent the majority of the units to Section 8 tenants. Some of the units may be converted to three bedrooms to increase the rents to about $450.00 per side rather than $375.00 per side. The cost to do this is about $1,000 per unit. Though demand for two-bedroom units is high, the demand for three-bedroom units is incredibly high.

The Section 8 Program

This program is for low-income families, mainly led by single mothers with children. The money is allotted for 10 years for each certificate holder or tenant by HUD and is administered by MDHA.

The leases are guaranteed for one year. Usually, the government pays all of the rent. Sometimes the tenant has to pay a small amount. MDHA inspects the units twice a year and requires them to be in good repair.

Section 8 and MDHA also insure against damages for up to two months' rent, about $750.00 for each unit. If the tenant damages the unit, the landlord can collect the damage money from Section 8.

The demand for available Section 8 housing is very high. Thus, I have been operating my 20 duplexes at a 100 percent occupancy rate with waiting lists for each property. The landlord can screen the tenants and does not have to rent to someone to whom he or she does not want to rent.

Financial Detail

Per-building purchase price	$39,000.00
18% down payment	7,020.00
Amount financed	31,980.00
Monthly payment, 15 years at 8.5% interest	314.92
Taxes per month	40.00
Insurance per month	25.00
Monthly payment with taxes and insurance	379.92
Current rent per duplex	750.00
Free cash flow per month	370.08

Risks

Vacancy and repair risks are inherent in real estate. The vacancy risk should be about zero. Again, the demand for Section 8 housing is high. I have not advertised in almost a year and have kept my 20 duplexes full. I get about 10 to 20 calls a week from people looking for housing. Furthermore, the Greenwood Project is in an excellent location. The repair cost is also minimal because Section 8 guarantees about two months' rent for damage repair. That is about $750.00 per unit. All of my appliances are insured, so it is very difficult for a tenant to do more than $750.00 worth of damage, especially if they are managed properly. Also, only one side of each duplex has to stay rented in order to pay the note, taxes, and insurance.

Management

I personally manage all of my properties. I walk through each unit at least once every 30 days. I have and intend to provide the highest-quality low- and moderate-income housing in Davidson County. All of my units are like new when the tenants move in, and I try to keep them that way.

I use licensed, bonded contractors for all of my repairs. They work for about $7.00 per hour and do quality work. Thus, whatever repairs I do incur are handled promptly, professionally, and reasonably.

Formulating a Winning Strategy

6 months	1 year	5 years	10 years	20 years

Personal goals, your health: _____

_____

Mental education: _____

_____

Spiritually: _____

_____

Family, you and your family: _____

_____

Vacation, travel plans: _____

_____

Fun, hobbies: _____

_____

Monetary, career: _____

_____

Charitable goals, helping others: _____

_____

Current job

Monthly income: _____   Annual income: _____

Current savings: _____   Current expenses: _____

Job satisfaction, 1–10: _____

Current credit: Excellent   Good   Fair   Bad

Investment savings

Car: _____

IRA: _____

Employee programs: _____

Cash: _____

Stocks/bonds: _____   Average yield: _____

Real estate: _____

Other: _____

Personality type

Analytical

Love to deal with people

Love to work with numbers, programs

Love to work with hands

Love to be alone

Great with big picture

Great with details

Available amount of money to invest in real estate

(Remember to keep a cushion)

Cash: _____   Brokerage loans: _____

Credit lines: _____   Private loans: _____

Equity line: _____   Family loans: _____

Unencumbered assets: _____   Credit cards (risky): _____

IRA: _____

Collateral to pledge for bank loans, real estate, stocks, bonds, and financial statements: _____

Banking relationship: _____

Income goals: _____

Cash flow for real estate wealth accumulation: _____

worksheet

	Annual Income Needs	Annual Income Goals	Actual Annual Income
Current	_____	_____	_____
1 year	_____	_____	_____
2 years	_____	_____	_____
3 years	_____	_____	_____
4 years	_____	_____	_____
5 years	_____	_____	_____
10 years	_____	_____	_____
15 years	_____	_____	_____
20 years	_____	_____	_____

Free hours, or hours available to spend on real estate weekly:

1–5   6–10   11–20   21–30   31–40   41–50   51–60   61–70   71–80

My Plan

Little or no capital/credit is required.

1. Flipping
   - Look at 20 houses.
   - Lock up three.
   - Flip one.
   - Average flip: $3,000 to $7,000.

2. Lease optioning
   - Call on 20 houses.
   - Negotiate with four.
   - Lease-option one.
   - Average monthly cash flow: $200 to $400.
   - Option profit: $500 to $3,000.
   - Beware of repair and vacancy.

3. Sandwich leasing
   - Call on 20 homes.
   - Negotiate with four.
   - Sandwich lease with two.
   - Monthly cash flow $100 to $400.

4. Mortgage brokering
   - Search, advertise for mortgages.
   - Find two decent ones.
   - Close on one.
   - Average brokerage commission: $1,500 to $5,000.
   - May need license.

5. Brokering tax certificates
   - Research local rules. Find investor, bid at auction for investors. Can be complicated. Liability can be high. May need license, though I could make substantial commissions and find great deals to flip.

6. Private money brokering (may need a license)
   - Find lenders, find good loans.
   - 1 to 5 percent spread per month.
   - 1 to 10 points up front.
   - Example: Broker a $40,000 loan (at 11 to 13 percent for a 15-year loan), 5 points = $2,000 up front, 2 percent spread at $60 per month for the life of the loan.

7. Flipping with taking back a note or cash and a note
   - Flip property, take back a second mortgage as my commission. Cash and monthly income.

8. Real estate agent (license needed)—commissions
   - Average commissions on a sale are 5 to 7 percent. I may have to split commission, plus pay my brokerage 20 to 70 percent of my commission. Sell a $100,000 house with a 6 percent commission and I earn $6,000. I may have to split with other agents and my broker.

9. Consulting
   - Consult with investors, retirees, nonprofits, governmental agencies, real estate firms, estates, attorneys, CPAs, and financial planners; give seminars. Promotion costs may be high. My fees: $35 to $200 per hour or commissions; flip potentials.

10. Property management
    - Need legal entity. Bank accounts, computer (preferably). Liability insurance $800 to $2,000 annually. Receive 8 to 11 percent of rents collected monthly. May keep late fees, charge tenants $50 to $150 application fee. Charge $50 to $150 lease renewal fee. Charge for and own my own maintenance company. May need to be a Realtor. Profits come with volume.

11. Maintenance company
    - Make ready empty units. Apartment get-ready. Fix up and clean apartments and houses. I can do it, or hire a subcontractor at $8 to $10 per hour or by the job. Painting, carpet cleaning, rehabilitation, landscaping.

12. Contract for deed/lease options
    - May be able to negotiate for little or no money down. I can control property, lease option, or contract for deed for more money per month. Get option/deposit money up front.

      Example: I can lease-option or contract for deed a house for $40,000, with $500 down, $400 per month for 20 years. I turn around and lease-option/contract and deed it for $1,500 down, $600 a month. I make a $1,000 profit up front, an additional $200 a month profit for the next 20 years. Average up-front profit: $500 to $5,000. Average monthly profit: $100 to $500. Little or no landlord headaches if done correctly.

Cash, capital, and/or credit may be required.

1. Buy, rehabilitate, and sell.
   - Need purchase money. May get owner's terms. Need money for repair costs and holding costs. Average rehab should net me at least $12,000, or about 30 percent of retail sales price. Alternative

to cash: Use investor's money, partner the deal, use equity sharing, or use credit lines.

2. Buy and hold real estate.
   - May need cash for down payment and repairs. Great wealth accu-
     mulator. Great cash flow each month. Rule of thumb: A single-
     family house should have a cash flow of at least $100 to $150 per
     month before vacancy and repairs, with a 65 to 75 percent loan on
     it.
   - Duplexes should cash-flow about $200 to $400 per month before
     vacancy and repairs. Multifamily units depend on capitalization
     rates, type, and size. Management can be a headache. I can hire a
     manager for between 7 and 11 percent of gross monthly rents.
     Great for cash flow and wealth accumulation.

3. Buy and create paper by creative selling.
   - I need cash or credit to buy and fix up. I then sell, taking some
     cash, a note, an installment deed, and/or a land contract. Gener-
     ates profits and cash flow. Beware of the tax burdens that come
     with the profits. My notes that I hold are marketable. I can sell
     them at discounts to raise cash. Good monthly income. Few, if
     any, management headaches.

index